THIS LAND WAS SAVED
FOR YOU AND ME

*How Gifford Pinchot, Frederick Law Olmsted, and a
Band of Foresters Rescued America's Public Lands*

JEFFREY H. RYAN

STACKPOLE
BOOKS
Essex, Connecticut
Blue Ridge Summit, Pennsylvania

STACKPOLE BOOKS

An imprint of Globe Pequot, the trade division of
The Rowman & Littlefield Publishing Group, Inc.
4501 Forbes Blvd., Ste. 200
Lanham, MD 20706
www.rowman.com

Distributed by NATIONAL BOOK NETWORK

British Library Cataloguing in Publication Information available

Library of Congress Cataloging-in-Publication Data

Names: Ryan, Jeffrey H., author.
Title: This land was saved for you and me : how Gifford Pinchot, Frederick Law Olmsted, and a
    band of foresters rescued America's public lands / Jeffrey H. Ryan.
Description: Guilford, Connecticut : Stackpole Books, [2022] | Includes bibliographical references
    and index.
Identifiers: LCCN 2022004578 (print) | LCCN 2022004579 (ebook) | ISBN 9780811771665
    (cloth) | ISBN 9780811771672 (epub)
Subjects: LCSH: Public lands—United States—History.
Classification: LCC HD216 .R93 2022 (print) | LCC HD216 (ebook) | DDC 333.10973—
    dc23/eng/20220504
LC record available at https://lccn.loc.gov/2022004578
LC ebook record available at https://lccn.loc.gov/2022004579

♾️™ The paper used in this publication meets the minimum requirements of American National
Standard for Information Sciences—Permanence of Paper for Printed Library Materials, ANSI/
NISO Z39.48-1992.

*To those who appreciate the significance
of our public lands and work to protect them.*

Love of wilderness is more than a hunger for what is always beyond reach. It is also an expression of loyalty to the earth, the earth which bore us and sustains us, the only home we shall ever know, the only paradise we ever need if only we had the eyes to see.

—EDWARD ABBEY

Man was made for broad scenes and tall shadows. He craves a noble background. Cramp him, and he revolves in an ever-narrowing circle, until he finally doubts his own destiny. The song goes out of his heart.

—ERNEST OBERHOLTZER

We are not fighting progress we are making it. We are not dealing with the vanishing wilderness. We are working for a wilderness forever.

—HOWARD ZAHNISER

Contents

Preface

I think I was largely educated for my profession by the enjoyment which my father and mother (step-mother) took in loitering journeys; in afternoon drives on the Connecticut meadows. This at first, help-ing to give me a bent, which . . . led me in long leisurely tramps and visits to friends on farms, to take a more intelligent, discriminating, analytical and cultivated interest in such scenery.[1]

—Frederick Law Olmsted

In 2016, I took my first steps on this hundred-year journey into our past. The quest has taken me physically and metaphorically to places across America and through decades of written history to learn about the people who championed the creation of and protection for our public lands.

What drove these pioneers to become such eloquent, impassioned voices for passing these enduring gifts to us? What role did their upbringing play? And having made great strides forward, whom did they entrust to carry the mission forward?

These questions compelled me to start following pathways back in time. Like most people, I suppose, I started by reading the biographies of these wondrous people. Over time, I began noticing how the story lines intersected like a family tree of conservation history. Sometimes the connections were fleeting. Often they were lasting. Yet the names and references kept leaping off the pages in unexpected ways. And the crusade to make our public lands accessible to all, not solely the monied interests, carried forth in a similarly interesting series of handoffs. A sheer dedication to and reverence for nature sustained these pioneers and inspired others to carry on.

Was it an acquired obsession? Was it developed through training and observation? Did all three come into play?

To find out, to paraphrase Gifford Pinchot, it was not enough to rely on historic documents alone. Thus I traveled to many of the places where the main characters in this tale were raised, worked, or were inspired to create the words and deeds they left in their wake—Pinchot's castle, where he spent many years formulating forestry policy; Yosemite Valley, where Olmsted made the case for protecting the land; Aldo Leopold's birthplace (in Iowa) and shack (in Wisconsin), where he set out to rehabilitate a piece of prairie; Benton MacKaye's childhood home and surroundings, where he discovered the restorative, life-sustaining qualities of nature; Ernest Oberholtzer's island in northern Minnesota, where he rallied neighbors and a nation to protect the Boundary Waters Canoe Area; and Howard Zahniser's childhood home near the Allegheny National Forest all beckoned me from afar.

I went because I wanted to affirm what I already suspected (and that Olmsted affirmed in the quote above). When we experience nature through the eyes of a child, we are often inspired to ensure that those who follow us can share that joy. And the best—in fact the only—way to make that happen is to work as hard as we can for it and inspire others to do the same.

One can't spend time in untrammeled places without feeling gratitude for those who made the protection of them possible. Olmsted, Pinchot, MacKaye, Bob Marshall, Leopold, Oberholtzer, Zahniser—every one of them enjoyed unforgettable childhood experiences in the outdoors. And every one had much to say about the importance of establishing and protecting wild lands—not as some kind of ageless museum, but as a place where we can reconnect with ourselves.

It is my hope that this story brings a wider appreciation for all the contributors who made, and make, America's wild lands an essential part of our ongoing saga, and that it inspires more people to discover, explore, and respect our public lands.

Portland, Maine
February 2022

Acknowledgments

I have two preferred modes of travel—on foot or by 1985 Volkswagen Vanagon. Friends often observe that both move at roughly the same speed. They have a point.

I am happiest when I am living at a pace that allows me to take in things more fully, if not conventionally, in this day of high-speed and extreme everything. Which brings me back to my Vanagon. Researching this book has taken me to some remarkable places. Sometimes it was to sift through archives (Knoxville, Tennessee, and the National Conservation Training Center in West Virginia come to mind), but more often it was to visit the places where America's conservation stories took root: Woodstock, Vermont; Rainy Lake, Minnesota; Tionesta, Pennsylvania; Burlington, Iowa; Baraboo, Wisconsin; Milford, Pennsylvania—the list goes on. Being in the places where George Perkins Marsh, Ernest Oberholtzer, Howard Zahniser, Aldo Leopold, Gifford Pinchot, and the other leaders of America's conservation movement were raised gave me a glimpse into why preserving the world around them was so important.

Along the way, I have met literally hundreds of researchers, restaurant owners, VW mechanics, good Samaritans, and well-wishers who have cheered me on. It's satisfying and humbling to know there are so many good people in this world willing to lend a hand.

It's always perilous to single a few people out, but I'd be remiss if I didn't thank Dr. Mark Madison, the talented and generous historian at the National Conservation Training Center; Rebecca Otto, executive director of the Ernest C. Oberholtzer Foundation; Buddy Huffaker, board president and executive director of the Aldo Leopold Foundation; and Mark Granlund, Minnesota artist extraordinaire, who have all helped me keep my research coordinates pointed in the right direction and leant their support.

CHAPTER ONE

Frederick Law Olmsted's Epiphany

IN JULY 1865, A FORTY-THREE-YEAR-OLD RODE A HORSE FROM A SWEL-tering, drought-stricken mining settlement to the pleasantly cool surroundings of Yosemite Valley to camp, fish, and explore the backcountry. It wasn't just the pleasing temperatures that compelled him to go there. It was to escape the daily pressure of running a gold mine.

Frederick Law Olmsted was not one to shun hard work or adventure. His life thus far had provided ample servings of both. The son of a successful Hartford, Connecticut, dry-goods owner had by turns been a surveyor, farmer, seafaring merchant, partner in a book publishing venture, reporter for the *New York Daily Times*, head of the Sanitary Commission (medical logistics coordinator) for the Union effort, and, most famously, the celebrated codesigner of New York's Central Park.

But running the Mariposa Company had been a struggle for most of the two years since he'd agreed to become its manager for the impressive annual salary of $10,000. It took Olm-sted less than a week to realize what a mess he'd stepped into. In a letter home to his wife, who with the family had stayed behind in New York, he said, "Things here are worse than I dare say to anyone but you."[1]

Frederick Law Olmsted, circa 1860. (Frederick Law Olmsted National Historic Site, National Park Service)

The situation was dire indeed. The former owners had luckily hit a productive vein of gold at precisely the time the mine was being evaluated for purchase, so the buyers believed the sustainable output would be steady and strong. But the vein quickly ran out. What's more, the former manager had stopped investing in the mine's infrastructure, so Olmsted was confronted with even greater challenges.

Managing the mine had been grueling from day one. His first tasks were to get the finances in order and get a true reading on what assets the company owned and whether a consistent path to profitability was even feasible. His days blurred together, but they generally involved having breakfast around noon and touring the mines with one or more of the eight crew supervisors under his employ or with a geologist he hired to survey the seventy-square-mile property. After dinner, he would often stay up until the wee hours of the morning going over the company's books. The relentless pressure and long days wore down his body and spirit. Olmsted, who was prone to bouts of depression, would sometimes go to San Francisco to speak with the bankers and stay for days to get away from the overwhelming pressure of attending to day-to-day profitability and its many masters.

The roller-coaster ride of profitable months and deficit-inducing months and the pressure of having to appease investors in New York and bankers in San Francisco proved overwhelming. Yet a trip to Yosemite Valley always offered a healthy respite.

Frederick Law Olmsted's first glimpse of the giant sequoias came barely a month after he arrived at the mine in the fall of 1863. He had immediately resolved that the fortunes of the Mariposa Company depended on the continuous flow of two commodities, gold and water. The stream that flowed through the company's property, like the mines themselves, was constantly in flux. The drought of 1863 had reduced it to barely a trickle. The surrounding land had withered to a dreary brown. In this lifeless, interminably dusty expanse, the mine's manager sprouted a grand plan. If he could divert the South Fork of the Merced River through the estate, "the constant water supply would not only prolong mining operations into the dry season but would permit agriculture and sheep raising on a large scale," which would in turn draw more year-round laborers to work on the estate, providing revenue through their payment of monthly rent.[2]

Fittingly, the man who would become the world's foremost landscape architect envisioned a vibrant, communal ecosystem, "an all-embracing relationship based on the confidence, respect and interest of each citizen in all and all in each."[3]

Everything hinged on his plan for a plentiful water supply, so in November 1863, he and a team of engineers set forth to find out if his plan could be achieved. Returning to Bear Valley five days later (the last day being a forty-mile ride on horseback), Olmsted wrote a detailed letter to the Mariposa Company's New York office. Yes, the canal was feasible, it could be a more profitable enterprise than he had envisioned, and it would cost around $1 million to build, he reported.[4]

While he was satisfied in affirming that his plan could set in motion a new era of profitability for the Mariposa Company (and its community of miners, shopkeepers, and settlers), he was overjoyed to share in a letter to his wife, Mary, another discovery he had made on the trip, the stunning beauty of the hills and groves surrounding the North Fork of the Merced. "I never saw and don't think you ever did, any tree to compare with the pines, cedars (arbor vitae) and firs, generally 200 to 250 feet high and as thrifty and dense and bright in foliage as saplings. Trunks of four feet are ordinary, of six feet not uncommon," he exclaimed.[5]

One month after submitting his glorious canal plan to the Mariposa Company board, they wrote back to report that his plan was well received but would have to wait. The company's payment of liens had reduced their working capital to a point where they needed to focus on production until they filled the coffers again, if ever.*

Olmsted remained as optimistic as he could about the company's viability. After all, some months were quite profitable, and he was able to stay ahead of the creditors. He even arranged for his extended family (including his wife, four children, a governess, and his wife's cousin

---

*The Mariposa canal was never built, but the subject of water management within the Yosemite Valley would become a contentious issue in the early 1900s when the Hetch Hetchy dam was proposed and built.

Henry Perkins, who would serve as Olmsted's secretary) to join him on the ranch in June 1864.

By mid-July, he was ready to introduce his family to the wonders of the Mariposa Grove and the valley beyond. He and an entourage including his family, a governess, a housekeeper, a cook, ten horses, eight mules, and two donkeys traveled forty miles to a ranch owned by Galen Clark.[6] From here, they took trips to see the giant sequoias, explore the valley, and fish the South Fork of the Merced River.

The several-week escape was invigorating. Camping across the verdant valley from Yosemite Falls, the highest waterfall in North America, with sheer granite walls rising straight up around him, Olmsted discovered something more precious than gold. It was a reverence for nature so powerful, so complete, that he was compelled to dash off a letter to his father. "The walls of the chasm [surrounding our camp] are a quarter of a mile distant, each side—nearly a mile in height—half a mile of perpendicular or overhanging rock in some places. Of course, it is awfully grand, but it is not frightful or fearful. It is sublimely beautiful, much more beautiful than I had supposed. The valley is as sweet & peaceful as the meadows of the Avon," he wrote.[7]

While Olmsted and his family were marveling at the Yosemite scenery, he was unaware that he would soon play the lead role in preserving it for all people and for all time.

In the spring of 1864, a California steamship executive named Israel Raymond had sent a letter and accompanying materials to John Conness, a U.S. senator representing the state, making the case that Yosemite needed to be protected. To make certain that the beauty of the area was not lost on the senator, Raymond included a set of spectacular stereographic prints taken by photographer Carleton Watkins (some of the first-known images of the valley) and a list of people whom Raymond felt were qualified to serve on a Yosemite Commission. Frederick Law Olmsted's name was one of them.[8]

When Olmsted (and family) returned to Bear Valley after their hiatus, there was a letter waiting for him. Unbeknownst to the manager of the Mariposa Company operations, Senator Conness's bill establishing Yosemite and the Mariposa Grove of giant sequoia trees as protected lands (and deeding them to the state of California) had passed in both chambers of the U.S. Congress and been signed into law by President Lincoln with remarkable speed. What's more, Olmsted had been named by the state's governor as a board member of the Yosemite Commission. At the first board meeting, Olmsted was voted in as its president.

Olmsted's first act was to have the boundaries of the park surveyed, paying the $500 out of his own pocket, since the commission had no budget. While Clarence King and James T. Gardiner set off to do their survey, Olmsted made his last effort to keep the Mariposa Company afloat.

It wouldn't be long before he'd be confronted by the reality that his management skills were no match for lawsuits and impatient creditors. In New York, one of the company's principal owners (a former New York City mayor) had sued a journalist for libel. The trial hadn't gone well for George Opdyke, who appeared to be as unsavory a businessman as advertised. The trial ended without a verdict, but the court of public opinion vilified Opdyke. His other business dealings, including an alleged scheme whereby he landed a Union army contract to provide blankets for the troops, had them constructed of inferior fabric, and pocketed the difference, had come out during the trial. The Mariposa Company stock price nose-dived. (In a happy coincidence, Olmsted, who knew nothing about the New York trial, had sold several hundred shares of Mariposa stock from his account well ahead of the proceedings.)

When three of the company's creditors arrived at the ranch with demands for immediate payment, Olmsted followed them back to San Francisco and arranged a one-hundred-day reprieve—a period during which he sent several inquiries to the company's owners, with no response. Finally, upon receiving a garbled telegram from the company's officers, Olmsted threw in the towel. He transferred the company's ownership to its largest creditor and determined that the end of his mining days was nigh.

Frederick Law Olmsted's two-year engagement as the manager of the Mariposa Company was not an abject failure. One of the reasons he took the job (perhaps the only one) was that he was $12,000 in debt—monies he owed his father and to the creditors of a publishing venture gone awry. When he left California, he would be out of debt and would have jobs awaiting him in the field he was most known for and would now dedicate his full ambition to—thanks to his former and soon-to-be-reestablished partner, Calvert Vaux.

But there was one important piece of business left. He invited his fellow commission members to Yosemite for a strategy session, where "Olmsted intended to make an oral report to his colleagues gathered around a campfire."[9] He hoped to gain consensus, fine-tune the report, and then send it to the California legislature to be formally enacted.

The Mariposa Report, as it would become known, would be the guide for creating a kind of park that had never been imagined—a place to be forever protected in its mostly wild state. Unlike the parks that would come to define the bulk of Olmsted's career, places where environments were created or improved upon (with bridges, drainage tiles, and other man-made infrastructure), places that brought nature closer to people, the call for Yosemite (and potentially other public lands) would be different. Here was a place where contemplative and recreational use were to be enjoyed because there was little intervention by man.

As biographer Elizabeth Stevenson noted, "Olmsted was aware, before many other people were, that these mountains and forests, which during millions of years of growth had taken shape without man's intervention, were now of first importance to man—if he could be brought to appreciate the wild."[10]

To be certain, a few notable pioneers had set the stage for Olmsted's bold plan. Ralph Waldo Emerson ("In the woods, we return to reason and faith") and Henry David Thoreau ("In wildness is the preservation of the world") had implored us to connect more fully with nature. Landscape artist Albert Bierstadt presented Yosemite's beauty quite literally in a new light. The area, which he described to a friend as a "Garden of Eden," inspired his ethereal 1864 painting *Valley of the Yosemite* and his soon-to-follow *Looking down Yosemite Valley, California* of 1865. In the photographic realm, Carleton E. Watkins's stereographic pictures (which Senator Conness had used to help garner support for the new park) presented Yosemite's grandeur to eager audiences across the country and beyond.

But Olmsted was charting a new course to ensure that the full measure of Yosemite could be enjoyed in person. He declared that Yosemite (as well as other special American lands) should be retained as the property of every citizen, and that the reason for doing so was not just to prevent the wealthy from having a monopoly on the most scenic areas in the country (although it was a major concern), but so that the areas could contribute to the spiritual and mental well-being of all who visited these treasured lands. He was quick to establish that "the enjoyment of scenery employs the mind without fatigue and yet exercises it, tranquilizes it and yet enlivens it; and thus, through the influence of the mind over the body, gives the effect of refreshing rest and reinvigoration of the whole system."[11]

The other critical underpinning of Olmsted's report was a mandate to preserve the proposed park's wild character as much as practicable. "The first point to be kept in mind," he wrote, "is the preservation and maintenance as exactly as is possible of the natural scenery; the restriction, that is to say, within the narrowest limits consistent with the necessary accommodation of visitors, of all artificial constructions and the prevention of all constructions markedly inharmonious with the scenery or which would unnecessarily obscure, distort or detract from the dignity of the scenery."[12]

Importantly, Olmsted stressed the need to protect the native plants and other natural features of the park from destruction in the name of generations to follow. Citing examples of thousands of people visiting the Alps and the overcrowded grand hotels in "the White Hills of New Hampshire," he foresaw a future when millions of visitors would come to Yosemite and urged the creation and strict enforcement of laws designed to protect and preserve the beauty that would inevitably draw people there.

To serve the anticipated crowds and to ensure that they would arrive at the park less fatigued and more able to enjoy its splendor, Olmsted proposed building a loop road with strategically placed turnouts that would safely accommodate visitors and service vehicles that could convey, among other things, firewood and food to visitors who were staying at the five cabins also proposed for the park. The anticipated cost for the road, cabins, footpaths, superintendent's salary for two years, and incidentals was $37,000.

On August 9, 1865, Olmsted unveiled his plan in the Yosemite Valley. In attendance were fellow commissioners Galen Clark and William Ashburner, along with several esteemed invitees who would ensure that the bold new plan would gain national attention, including reporters from the *New York Tribune* and *Chicago Tribune*.

Also present was an intriguing traveling duo that had garnered a national following. Speaker of the U.S. House Schuyler Colfax (who would go on to become vice president under U. S. Grant) had been making his way west on a well-publicized nationwide jaunt that had originally been planned to commemorate the first ride of the Pony Express in 1860. Delayed by the Civil War, Colfax now attempted his transcontinental adventure accompanied by Samuel Bowles, the publisher of one of the largest circulating daily newspapers in New England, the *Springfield Republican* (the moniker Bowles had suggested for the new political party he helped launch in 1855), and a close friend of Emily Dickinson. In an era when reporting tended to be long-winded, Bowles advocated brevity and would exhort his reporters to "put it all in the first paragraph."[13]

After four days of exploring Yosemite and taking in the sights, Samuel Bowles was overwhelmed. "The Yosemite!" he gushed. "As well interpret God in thirty-nine articles as portray it to you by word of mouth or pen. As well reproduce castle or cathedral by a stolen frieze, or broken column, as this assemblage of natural wonder and beauty by photograph or painting. . . . It was Niagara, magnified. All that was mortal shrank back, all that was immortal swept to the front and bent down in awe."[14]

Samuel Bowles, circa 1888.
(Photographer unknown)

As Olmsted presented his findings to the esteemed gathering in Yosemite, he hoped that his eight-thousand-word report would similarly inspire his audience and, eventually, the California legislature. What he didn't know was that his efforts would be undermined from within. Three members of the Yosemite Commission were concurrently serving as commissioners of the California Geological Survey. Because CGS funding was also at stake, they couldn't (or wouldn't) justify the Yosemite Commission's requests for support. The trio even convinced Governor Low to suppress Olmsted's report and, as a result, the $37,000 budgetary request to fund its implementation.[15]

Yet a few important pieces of Olmsted's plan still moved ahead. After several fits and starts, Galen Clark (aka "Guardian of the Grant"), a longtime resident of the valley who had served on the Yosemite Commission, successfully led the charge to build an access road (known as the Wawona Road) into Yosemite to make it easier for tourists to view the sights (and stay at his camps).

Samuel Bowles's account of his journey, *Across the Continent: A Summer's Journey to the Rocky Mountains, the Mormons and the Pacific States with Speaker Colfax*, also sought to keep Olmsted's vision in the public eye. After describing the features of Yosemite ("the highest rock of the Valley is a perfect half-dome"), he praised "the laudable and promising effort" led by Frederick Law Olmsted to secure funds for improving access, creating trails, providing "cheap accommodations for visitors," and protecting the land for the public benefit. Bowles then asked his readers to imagine an even grander vision. Olmsted's Yosemite plan "furnishes an admirable example for other objects of natural curiosity and popular interest all over the Union," Bowles wrote. "New York should preserve for popular use both Niagara Falls and its neighborhood and a generous section of her famous Adirondacks, and Maine one of her lakes and surrounding woods."[16]

In 1865, Bowles's book (and to a much larger degree, his articles) was read by a nation still raw from four years of enduring struggle, followed by the shocking assassination of President Lincoln. Emerging from its state of grief, the union rallied around a sense of national purpose. Ideas, institutions, and infrastructure were rapidly becoming national in scope. "National banks were superseding state banks; national securities were a favorite investment. A railroad was being constructed to bind one end of the nation to the other, and eastern capital poured into the development of western resources."[17]

Frederick Law Olmsted's vision for Yosemite exuded that sense of national purpose. It was a plan that looked toward a day when millions of visitors would pour in annually to see and feel what Galen Clark, Olmsted, Samuel Bowles, and others so wanted to share and protect, a gift to the nation and the world to last for eternity. In fact, it was the precursor in both tenor and practice for all the federal lands to follow.

Yet the credit due Olmsted for establishing Yosemite as the birthplace of the national park idea would diminish, to be replaced with an alternate version of history, namely that Yellowstone was the birthplace of the national park idea (and ideal). One reason that Olmsted's role was overlooked is that he left California to pursue other projects and was no longer involved or otherwise affiliated with Yosemite. A greater reason was that other than "the description of the special landscape qualities of Yosemite Valley that [Olmsted] published in the *New York Evening Post* of June 18, 1868; the [Mariposa Report] itself was lost to the world for the following half century."[18] It would not be until 1916, when Frederick Law Olmsted Jr. was looking for inspirational phrases among his father's writings that the younger might use in his role as a contributor to the creation of the national park system, that the original Mariposa Report surfaced.

Published many times since then, the report reaffirmed Frederick Law Olmsted's foresight in advocating for public lands, specifically national parks to be enjoyed by all. In 1948, national parks historian Dr. Hans Huth wrote an article titled "Yosemite: The Story of an Idea," which would be published in the *Sierra Club Bulletin*. In the foreword accompanying the piece, *Bulletin* editor David Brower stated, "Dr. Huth has made it imperative that future historians abandon the common assumption that the national park idea was born at a campfire in Yellowstone in 1870. Six years before that campfire, Congressional action had already been taken to set aside Yosemite Valley, that it might be enjoyed in perpetuity as a scenic resource for all the people."[19]

In the article itself, Huth shared with readers that the Yosemite grant bill that was passed and signed into law on June 29, 1864, by President Lincoln,

was destined to set a precedent of real importance. The grant was given "upon the express conditions that the premises shall be held for

public use, resort and recreation, shall be held inalienable for all time."
These terms implied that no profit was to be expected from the new
institution. . . . What was really new about the grant was the fact
that it served a strictly nonutilitarian purpose. It is necessary to stress
this point in view of the claims that Yellowstone set this precedent.[20]

Of course, those conditions were introduced by Olmsted, whose report
stipulated, "It is the will of the nation as embodied in the act of Congress
that this scenery shall never be private property, but that like certain defen-
sive points upon our coast it shall be held solely for public purposes."[21]

As Brower noted in the foreword to Huth's subsequent book, the case
for securing Yosemite as a public resource for its scenic and recreational
qualities and the public's benefit was made six years before the Yellowstone campfire discussion of 1870. But perhaps more important histori-
cally is that the case was made by Olmsted himself, whose explorations
of the valley inspired his call for its protection. As Huth wrote in 1948,

The coincidence of Olmsted's arrival in California at the very moment
when he was most needed has curiously enough never been noticed.
For once it seems that the right man was in the right spot at the right
time. Living in Mariposa, Olmsted was in close touch with Yosemite.
. . . Certainly no one was better prepared to take an active part in
urging the Yosemite grant and to keep the ball rolling.[22]

Squelched by political opportunists in California and drawn back
east in the name of employment, Olmsted's ability to "keep the ball rolling" had been compromised. But his call to establish Yosemite as a great
public ground "for the free enjoyment of the people"—a place where they
could revel in beauty, "find relief from ordinary cares," and gain the benefits of contemplation and recreation—would be rediscovered to secure
Olmsted's place as a powerful voice for national parks created and then
protected in the name of the people. As he said in the Mariposa Report,
"this duty of preservation is the first which falls upon the state under the
Act of Congress, because the millions who are hereafter to benefit by the
Act have the largest interest in it, and the largest interest should be first
and most strenuously guarded."[23]

CHAPTER TWO

Happily Associated Passages
of Natural Scenery

WHEN THE INCESSANT UNCERTAINTY OF RUNNING THE MARIPOSA Company extended beyond what Olmsted could be expected to handle in the field—when liens and lawsuits became as much of the burden as finding and extracting gold—he began casting about for other forms of employment.

Fortunately, his reputation as the originator of Central Park had prospects approaching him. The city of Oakland, California, hired him to create a cemetery on a hillside. He had also been contacted by the California university system to design a campus for a new facility to be located in what would be called Berkeley. Those two projects gave Olmsted sources of immediate income, but he wasn't yet certain that he wanted to continue to be known as a landscape architect.

In his younger days, Olmsted had been somewhat of a wandering worker in search of a career. Largely funded by his father, he had spent time as a surveyor, then a commercial farmer, specializing in growing fruit for customers in New York City. Taking a break from farming, he had become a deckhand on a cargo ship bound to China and back, a journey that lasted almost a year.

The farm took a backseat again between 1852 and 1854, when the *New York Daily Times* hired Olmsted to write a series about slavery in the American South. His brother, John, joined him for the trip. The articles Olmsted submitted from the road were so popular that upon his return he began writing a book about his adventures. This in turn set several wheels in motion. *Putnam's Monthly Magazine* had been sold to two young entrepreneurs (Joshua Dix and Arthur Edwards), who approached Olmsted with a partnership opportunity.

The chance to buy into the popular monthly magazine held allure for Olmsted. Instead of writing articles for other publications, he could share in the profits of writing for one he co-owned. Dix and Edwards also planned to expand into book publishing and told Olmsted that the project he was working on, a book about his experiences in the slave states, "would be a perfect fit."[1] Becoming a part owner would practically ensure his ability to sustain a writing career and provide stability.

It was an offer too compelling for Olmsted to ignore. He considered selling his farm to raise capital, but it would not generate nearly enough of the $5,000 needed. Thus, a family solution was hatched whereby Olmsted's dear brother John, who was ill with tuberculosis, would move to the farm with his family, and John Olmsted, the father, would lend the money to his son under the condition that it would be paid back.

It took less than a year for things to start unraveling. By the time Olmsted completed his manuscript for *A Journey in the Seaboard Slave States* in November 1855, *Putnam's* was unable to bear the cost of printing it. He borrowed $500 more from his father to pay for the print run of two thousand copies.

The magazine's circulation continued to wane, as did its chances for survival. Eventually, Olmsted's partners dissolved the company and sold it to a new investor. Olmsted believed there was at least a slim chance it would stay afloat.

In the face of this uncertainty, Olmsted didn't give up on his career as an author. Not just yet, anyway. Instead, he went to a seaside Connecticut hotel to work on his next book, tentatively called *A Journey in the Back Country*, also about his southern travels. It was at the hotel that he received a letter from *Putnam's* publisher, George Curtis, informing him that the firm had collapsed and declared bankruptcy. The six words, "We failed today. It was unavoidable," conveyed the abruptness of the firm's demise.

As he sat alone in the hotel sipping tea, Olmsted's prospects seemed bleak. He owed his father $5,500 and desperately needed an immediate source of income. Neither farming nor writing would be his salvation. He had no idea that the man who would change his life was about to enter the room.

An acquaintance, Charles Elliott, who had checked into the hotel recognized Olmsted and struck up a conversation. The two had met several years before and shared many interests, including landscape design and writing. Elliott had written for *Putnam's*, so the magazine's failure was a conversation starter. What Olmsted didn't know was that Elliott was also a newly minted member of the Board of Commissioners of the Central Park. Elliott told Olmsted that the park was in immediate need of a superintendent and urged him to apply for the job.

That night, Olmsted boarded a ferry bound for New York City, wondering whom he could or should contact as references. His hustling for support worked. Within weeks, he was supervising a workforce in the field, but it was without the benefit of a firm plan. For even before Olmsted was hired, the commission had decided that the plan for the park needed work itself. To generate new ideas, the commission had launched a design contest. The winning designer(s) would become the new lead architects for the park, and the work would be performed to their specifications. (In the spirit of fairness, the park's initial architect was invited to either resubmit his existing plan or to submit a new one to become part of the competition.)

One designer who was vitally interested in submitting a plan was a man Olmsted had met years before, Calvert Vaux. At the age of nineteen, Vaux had become known in his native London for his ability to restore Gothic churches. Upon moving to America, he'd been hired by landscape architect Andrew Jackson Downing, with whom he cre-

Calvert Vaux, before 1920.
(Unattributed photo)

ated several high-profile projects, including a "150-acre garden between the Capitol and the Washington Monument in Washington, D.C."[2]

Why Vaux reached out to Olmsted is subject to historical debate. What is certain is that Olmsted brought both his intimate knowledge of the park's topography and his writing skills to the table. More significantly, he brought a revolutionary vision—to champion nature's beauty over man-made buildings, monuments, and roads.

Olmsted and Vaux's winning proposal (which they named "Greensward") was easily the most detailed of the entries and included insights that Olmsted would include in his Yosemite report six years later—the projected growth of the city (and thus, visitors to the park) and the need for the park to be an oasis where all citizens could reconnect with the natural world. Olmsted and Vaux invited commissioners to envision a time when the park would be surrounded by "a continuous high wall of brick, stone, and marble," when "the town will have enclosed the Central Park."[3] Because of this, they made the case for minimizing the existence of man-made structures by limiting their use or obscuring sightlines.

> *The visitor, who, in the best case is the true owner . . . should concentrate on features of natural, in preference to artificial, beauty. Many elegant buildings may be appropriately erected for desirable purposes in a public park, but we conceive that all such architectural structures should be confessedly subservient to the main idea, and that nothing artificial should be obtruded on the view as an ultimatum of interest. The idea of the park itself should always be uppermost in the mind of the beholder.*[4]

The importance of making scenery the primary aspect of park design (as opposed to sidewalks, statues, and other man-made features) was an idea that took root when Olmsted was a child, during family sojourns to the Green Mountains of Vermont, the White Mountains of New Hampshire, and as far west as Niagara Falls.[5] Olmsted historian Charles E. Beveridge observed that "as he developed his theory of landscape design, Olmsted became convinced that scenery had a particularly beneficial effect on the human psyche, an effect both relaxing and restorative," and that "for Olmsted, the gift of soothing relaxation was the highest contribution that the art of landscape architecture could provide to mankind."[6]

The "gift of soothing relaxation" would, of course, be the lasting gift of Olmsted's designs and become a guiding principle of those who became his direct and indirect disciples for retaining and protecting public lands.

When it came to Central Park, Olmsted's growing concern was that his design would need to be realized without the benefit of his day-to-day oversight. Beginning in May 1858, Olmsted was named architect in chief and superintendent, with Vaux serving as consulting architect. Things went generally well until a commissioner named Andrew Haswell Green insisted on imposing "his ideas and strict control upon the park" and wishing "every cent spent on Central Park to be accounted for to him."[7] Olmsted continually bristled at the arrangement, feeling it was an affront to his ability to get necessary work done, despite holding titles "that implied specific and large responsibilities and the power to discharge them. The comptroller had effectively stripped him of power: through his tenaciously held financial control, Green was the absolute czar of the park."[8] In the face of ongoing squabbles, Olmsted attempted to resign, only to be walked back by the commissioners.

Finally, by June 1861, Olmsted was convinced to join the Union effort in the Civil War. Taking a three-month leave from his Central Park duties, he accepted the role of the executive secretary of the U.S. Sanitary Commission. Providing logistical support in getting hospital supplies to Union troops eased his departure financially and emotionally—as a vocal abolitionist, he enthusiastically supported the effort. But as the army began to assume many functions of the Sanitary Commission, Olmsted saw an opportunity to resign. In August 1863, Olmsted accepted the Mariposa Company's offer that would take him to California—thousands of miles away from the front lines of the still raging war and the turf battles with comptroller Green that had forced him to leave his beloved Central Park.

During the spring and summer of 1865, while Olmsted was ensconced in the Golden State drafting his Yosemite report, and concurrently working on his cemetery and university campus proposals, he was also being wooed back into the fold by Calvert Vaux, who sent a number of letters imploring Olmsted to come back east to partner with him again. Olmsted put Vaux off. Vacillating between protesting and not responding, Olmsted bought enough time for him and his wife, Mary, to investigate investing in a California oil venture or starting a winery. His protestations to Vaux were colored by his experience of being micromanaged by Commissioner Green and referenced Olmsted's poor health in the wake of the Mariposa Company ordeal. In a March 12, 1865, letter, he wrote,

> *My heart really bounds (if you don't mind poetry) to your suggestion that we might work together. . . . I can't tell you, and you can't conceive how I would like to expect it. But I don't think it likely. My health is weak.*[9]

But in the end, Vaux won out. He had two projects waiting. One was Olmsted's reappointment as the landscape architect of Central Park; the other was to codesign Brooklyn's Prospect Park—an enormous undertaking that would reestablish Olmsted and Vaux as the world's preeminent landscape architects.

Between 1858 and 1872, Olmsted and Vaux would work on more than forty projects together, including the Capitol grounds, numerous college and university campuses, and dozens of public parks in cities from coast to coast. Yet one of those projects offered a singular opportunity for Olmsted to approach "questions of scenic value in the same way he had at Yosemite"[10]—the Niagara Reservation.

ONE OF THE GREAT TREASURES OF THE WORLD

In 1869, Olmsted visited Niagara with the intention of garnering support to preserve its scenic qualities before the opportunity slipped away. He, as well as a few Buffalo-area civic-minded businessmen were concerned that the existing mishmash of industry- and tourism-related structures were setting the stage for wholesale development that would destroy the very character of the place. Olmsted later recounted the meeting of concerned citizens by drawing a parallel to his effort championing the scenic qualities of Yosemite, writing, "I had shortly before been engaged

Niagara Falls. (Library of Congress)

in establishing the State Reservation of California for the preservation and free Public use of the natural scenery of the Yosemite Valley and the Mariposa Grove and the question had been on my mind whether something should not be done with a similar purpose at Niagara."[11]

During Olmsted's 1869 visit, he toured Goat Island in the Niagara River above the falls and discussed the encroachment of industry, its devastating effects on the surroundings, and the need to do something about it with prominent business leaders who shared his concern. But it would be another decade before anything was done about it.

By 1879, the effort to establish Niagara Falls and its surroundings as a publicly owned entity had gained enough support to warrant further investigation. The commissioners of the state survey (those charged with mapping the Empire State) were instructed and authorized by a joint resolution of the New York legislature to "inquire, consider and report what, if any, measures it may be expedient for the State to adopt for carrying out the suggestions contained in the annual message of the Governor, with respect to Niagara Falls." Notably, the directive also included authorization to "confer with any commission or other authorized body, person or person representing the Dominion of Canada or the Province of Ontario, making a similar inquiry or contemplating measures for a similar purpose."[12]

While Olmsted drew on his experience of protecting Yosemite's grandeur to present a similar case for Niagara Falls, there was one significant difference. In Yosemite Valley, human impact had been minimal (ironically in part because Olmsted's original plan for building a million-dollar canal had not been realized). Conversely, the mission at Niagara Falls would include removing existing structures that compromised the serenity and beauty that would otherwise be the defining characteristics of the site—a point driven home in the first paragraphs of the report, which was presented in March 1880.

> *Under the resolution it became the duty of the Commissioners to ascertain how far the private holding of land about Niagara Falls has worked to public disadvantage through defacements of the scenery; to determine the character of such defacements; to estimate the tendency to greater injury; and lastly, to consider whether the proposed action by the State is necessary to arrest the process of destruction and restore the scenery to its original character.*[13]

As to how much damage had been already done, the commissioners Gardner and Olmsted argued that "the scenery of Niagara Falls has been greatly injured, that the process of injury is continuous and accelerating, and that, if not arrested, it must in time be utterly destructive of its value."[14]

In advocating for the removal of the jumble of industrial and commercial buildings lining the shores of the Niagara River, Olmsted revisited a theme from the Yosemite Commission report—that the need for unmarred scenery, places that engendered a "composed, receptive and contemplative mind," were essential to our well-being.[15] Further, he wrote, it was the duty of New York's legislators to ensure Niagara was restored and preserved for generations to come.

> *It cannot be debated that another generation will hold us greatly to account if we so neglect or so hastily administer our trust that the Falls of Niagara lose their beauty and their human interest. If we blame the*

men of a former day for not setting apart when it was the property of the State and might easily have been done, the Falls of Niagara as the Yo Semite and the Yellowstone have in our day been set apart, then how much more culpable shall we be, who knowing their value and perceiving their certain destruction, still refuse to take the necessary measures for their preservation.[16]

It would take another three years and a spirited public campaign featuring a petition signed by more than seven hundred citizens, including Charles Darwin, Ralph Waldo Emerson, John Ruskin, Thomas Carlyle, and Henry Wadsworth Longfellow, to convince then governor of New York Grover Cleveland to sign the bill that culminated in the creation of the Niagara Reservation.

In the span of less than twenty years, Frederick Law Olmsted had been instrumental in securing the permanent protection of two of America's most wondrous places—Yosemite and Niagara Falls. More than that, he established the primal, spiritual need for humans to be in nature's thrall as a primary reason to protect the land and be its benevolent steward.

It isn't surprising that Olmsted understood the vital need to connect with nature and the ability to advocate for it. At the time the Niagara Reservation was officially created, he had spent over sixty years surveying, cultivating, and observing the land from the posh gardens of Europe to the mountains of California and had traveled by train, horse, and steamship from the largest cities in China to the dry plains of Texas. He had a yen for contemplation, an eye for natural beauty, and a gift for writing. There is no doubt that his ample and diverse life experiences allowed him to understand that nature's handiwork rarely benefited from the heavy hand of humans. As one researcher noted, "Perhaps it was because Olmsted was the best, or most successful, craftsman of his time in the art of landscape architecture in this country that he could appreciate the value of the most breath-taking scenery of North America,"[17] and that he knew—and let it be known—that nature's design was the grandest of all.

By the end of the 1880s, Olmsted was poised to begin the most prolific and celebrated phase of his career—one that would once again influence the creation and protection of public lands in profound and not always obvious ways.

CHAPTER THREE

Birthplace of American Forestry

BY 1890, FREDERICK LAW OLMSTED WAS DIVIDING HIS TIME BETWEEN two projects that, along with Central Park, would comprise his life's three crowning achievements.

Two years prior, he had been summoned to Asheville, North Carolina, by George Vanderbilt, a fourth-generation descendent of Cornelius Vanderbilt, the shipping and railroad magnate, to "advise him what to do with an estate he was at this time secretly purchasing, buying up acres upon acres through an agent, so that he might assemble a large aggregation of land without exciting the local sellers."[1]

When Olmsted first viewed the property, he immediately envisioned the potential for turning much of the formerly clear-cut land back into a forest that could be managed for production. He advised his client that the grounds closest to the main house could be utilized to create formal gardens and farmland where he could "fatten livestock with an eye toward manure."[2] After taking a few months to think about it, Vanderbilt embraced the plan and Olmsted went to work.

The recommendation to reforest the land was a bold one, for Olmsted was one of just a few Americans advocating the need to manage forests as national assets. His extensive travels across varied landscapes nationwide and his ability to see into the future undoubtedly shaped this view. As biographer Justin Martin noted, "During recent travels he had grown conscious of a myth: America the primeval land of limitless forest. From train-car windows and stagecoaches, he'd noted what big timber was doing, clear-cutting huge stretches of land. The proto-environmentalist in

Biltmore House, circa 1902. (Detroit Publishing Company photograph collection, Library of Congress)

Olmsted, the same side that led him to become involved in Yosemite and Niagara Falls, drew him to this issue."[3]

But there were a few sage individuals who also shared a sense of urgency toward replanting and managing large tracts of forests. Olmsted was likely aware of the writings of George Perkins Marsh, whose book *Man and Nature*, published in 1864, ranked second only to Darwin's *On the Origin of Species* as the most influential book on nature of its time. Marsh passionately advocated for sustainable practices in farming and in forestry, a profession that existed only in Europe at the time his book was published.

One of Olmsted's contemporaries, Horace Cleveland (often referred to as the second most famous landscape architect of their era), had recently written his own booklet on forestry titled *The Culture and Management of Native Forests for the Development of Timber or Ornamental Wood*. We know for sure that Olmsted knew about Cleveland's booklet—he sent a copy to George Vanderbilt, which helped convince him to reforest the bulk of his land because he "liked the idea of harvesting timber on his property; that would provide a source of income," and "he was intrigued by the notion of a showcase for managed forestry."[4]

Another man who was deeply moved by the call for new forestry practices was a Pennsylvania entrepreneur (and friend of Frederick Law Olmsted) named James Wallace Pinchot, who had made millions of dollars through importing, then later manufacturing, Victorian wallpapers.

James Pinchot was a proponent of public service. He was instrumental in securing the design and construction of the pedestal for the Statue of Liberty. He was also a principal benefactor of both the National Academy of Design and the American Museum of Natural History. But his greatest contribution to America was made in the development of forestry as a profession. Pinchot was influenced so greatly by George Perkins Marsh's book *Man and Nature* that he convinced his son Gifford to pursue a career in silviculture. While attending Yale University, his son, who was already boasting "to incredulous peers that forestry would become his lifework,"[5] was assured by a professor of agriculture that there was not a single American university that included forestry in its curriculum.

Gifford's response was not one of disappointment but optimism. He wrote a letter to his father regarding the implications of his inquiry: "I shall have not only no competitors, but even a science to found."[6]

Upon graduating from Yale, and with his parents' backing, Gifford Pinchot set sail for Europe, where he would meet with the most renowned foresters of the day and attend the esteemed L'Ecole Nationale Forestiere in Nancy, France.[7] After one year of intense study in the classroom and in the field

Gifford Pinchot, circa 1909. (Library of Congress online collection)

(which he believed far more valuable), the young forester returned to America, driven in large part by his desire to make his profession a national priority before someone else did.

After writing several articles for Charles S. Sargent's *Garden and Forest* (a national publication read largely by forestry professionals) and appearing as a headline speaker at the 1890 joint session of the annual American Economic Association and American Forestry Association meetings, Pinchot would discover that America wasn't quite ready to embrace his vision for managing forests.

But Olmsted was. He convinced his patron, George Vanderbilt, that the young man was just the person to revitalize the vast landholdings surrounding what would be his hilltop estate. In addition to being a friend of James Pinchot, Olmsted was almost certainly familiar with the younger Pinchot's aspirations through additional sources. Charles Sargent, whose magazine Gifford had written a series of articles for, was also the man who had come up with the idea for Harvard's Arnold Arboretum, an Olmsted client.

Because of Pinchot's efforts at the Biltmore Estate, the hallowed ground is credited with being the birthplace of American forestry. There is no question that Gifford Pinchot orchestrated a forest revival on Vanderbilt's massive estate, that it was the first large-scale demonstration of a working forest in America, and that the project brought desperately needed attention to forestry as a profession. But the *idea* for the Biltmore forestry project was not Pinchot's. It was Olmsted's.

Historian Char Miller observed that "Olmsted, after all, had created the intellectual and cultural context for the younger man's work on the estate: it was he who launched the topographical survey of the estate that Pinchot would extend."[8] It was also Olmsted who encouraged his patron, Vanderbilt, to build small gardens near the manse and to establish the rest of his holdings as working forest more than two years before Pinchot's hiring.

This is not to diminish Pinchot's contribution to forestry. Gifford Pinchot deserves credit for being both a pioneer of American forestry and one of the greatest influences on the creation of and uses for our public lands. But at the Biltmore, he wasn't yet acting in the role of a visionary. Rather, he was building and refining a design that had been handed to him by a benefactor who believed in him—his father's acquaintance, Mr. Olmsted. Pinchot needed a place to put his newly acquired skills into practice, and Olmsted had just the place and person in mind to do it—yet another of Olmsted's wise decisions.

In 1891, with the Biltmore project well underway and Pinchot directing forest-related activities on site, Olmsted turned his attention to Chicago to oversee the other project that would bring him international acclaim—the World's Columbian Exposition of 1893.

Chapter Four

Triumph and Tragedy

One of Olmsted's most celebrated projects was one he initially shied away from. It is just one of the several ironies surrounding the World's Columbian Exposition of 1893. Suddenly a man who reshaped landscapes by envisioning what they would look like decades into the future found himself creating an environment that upon completion would only exist for six months. When the fair closed its doors, almost everything would be taken away, to live on only in memory and photographs.

Olmsted had determined that the only way he could add the fair to his ever-increasing workload was to keep his twenty-seven-year-old protégé, Henry Codman, working full time in Chicago, while he shuttled between the other projects. Despite the workload (and maybe because of it, as the man barely slept and was always physically or mentally in motion), he continued to turn majestic visions into reality. For the Biltmore, he designed a three-mile driveway rising through an ever-changing forest landscape that obscured the Richard Morris Hunt–designed mansion until finally emerging to reveal it at once in jaw-dropping splendor.

For the World's Columbian Exposition of 1893, Olmsted's challenge was the opposite. The grounds would feature spectacular Beaux Arts–style buildings designed by lead architect Daniel Burnham, who along with Olmsted conceived a stunning achievement. Olmsted, worried that the bright white facades of the buildings showcased at the fair might be visually too arresting, designed several water features into the grounds, including enormous lagoons to reflect the sky. But his vision

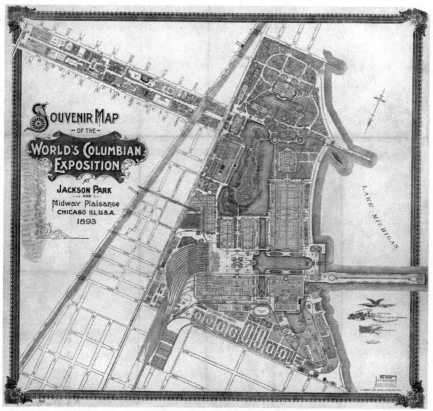

Souvenir map of the World's Columbian Exposition showing pools and green spaces designed by Olmsted. (Library of Congress)

for the ample use of foliage was inspired. Olmsted called for creating "an agreeable foreground over which the great buildings of the Exposition [would] rise," making them appear even more lofty and grand than they would without the plantings.[1]

Yet there was another reason Olmsted was championing the need for foliage, one with a higher sense of purpose—"to establish a considerable extent of broad and apparently natural scenery, in contemplation of which a degree of quieting influence will be had, counteractive to the effect of the artificial grandeur and the crowds, pomp, splendor and bustle of the rest of the Exposition."[2]

27

One such oasis was a wooded island accessed by a walkway, where fairgoers could relax. With exhibitor space at a premium, the island, originally designed by Olmsted to have no man-made structures on it at all, was under pressure to "be developed." Even Theodore Roosevelt got in on the act, envisioning building a hunting camp to showcase his Boone and Crockett Club, to which "Olmsted gave a flat no." But the clamoring for island space didn't cease until he agreed to let the Japanese government build a replica of a low-rise Kyoto temple more in keeping with the scenery. One young Chicago architect, an assistant to Louis Sullivan, would be particularly inspired by the temple's design. His name was Frank Lloyd Wright.[3]

To add a final colorful yet practical flourish, Olmsted ordered electric launches with brightly colored canvas tops to shuttle fairgoers between exhibits and allow them to take a break from walking the six-hundred-acre grounds. The other fair directors had pushed back against this idea, lobbying for larger-capacity launches, but Olmsted prevailed, which it was later agreed added a fun and exciting air that would have been missed.

Another thing Olmsted needed to prevail over was Henry Codman's unexpected death following an appendectomy in February 1893. With less than two months remaining before the grand opening, the grand designer rushed back to Chicago, intending "to throw everything into a final sprint in Chicago, but he wondered if it would kill him."[4] At age seventy, he gave it his all, fighting through bouts with insomnia, frigid winter days on the job site, and everything else required to make the May 1893 fair opening date a reality.

In all, over 40,000 workers helped build the fair's "14 main buildings (enclosing 63 million square feet), food and drink concessions, numerous smaller buildings, and an 80 acre 'Midway Plaisance' containing carnival-style rides and attractions. The construction consumed more than 75 million board feet of lumber, 18,000 tons of iron and steel, 120,000 incandescent lights, and 30,000 tons of staff—a type of white plaster facade that encased many of the buildings and earned the fair its 'White City' nickname."[5]

The fair opened on May 1, 1893. After a slow start that was attributed to poor spring weather, the exposition was an astounding success. Over one hundred thousand people attended the opening, and over twenty-seven million people visited the fair over the six months it was open.[6]

There were many reasons for the fair's success. Technological advances alone drew people by the millions. At night, the magnificent buildings were illuminated by more than ninety thousand lights, such that the energy used to light the fair was three times that used to illuminate all of Chicago.[7] A dedicated communications department promoted the fair as an event worth experiencing and remembering—a true media event that continued to build from itself.

Daniel Burnham, director of works for the fair, had a clear idea of what he wanted fairgoers to experience from the outset, but Olmsted's contributions brought forth a profound and unexpected realization. "The World's Fair," Burnham would later reflect, "disclosed what all were unconsciously waiting to receive, a lesson in landscape architecture. What the matter was with our public improvements, the Columbian Exposition made forever plain. Here, studied on the spot by millions, and by millions more through the activities of the Bureau of Publicity and Promotion, a great truth, set forth by great artists, was taught to all our people. This truth is the supreme one of the need of design and plan for whole cities."[8]

What the millions of visitors experienced was certainly a vision of what was possible, but it was also a temporary one. As one historian observed, "It was a land of enchantment free from pain and poverty, with beautiful marble-like buildings, basins, avenues, palaces of consumption, spectacles, entertainments and wonders."[9] Few of the 1893 fairgoers could imagine the tragedy that was playing out in the shadows of the optimistic, wondrous, and mostly temporary city on Lake Michigan.

In 1889, Frederick Law Olmsted received a proposal for a building so audacious that he declared, "This is the noblest artistic scheme I have ever heard of. It will be the crowning glory of the Fair, and all connected with it ought to feel deeply in debt to Mr. MacKaye for his creation. Such a conception deserves the place of honour on the Exposition Grounds."[10]

The gentleman he was referring to was "likely the greatest *unknown* theater inventor, playwright, designer, teacher, innovator and impresario ever,"[11] Steele MacKaye (pronounced Mac-EYE). Steele MacKaye's rise to American (and international) prominence had been built through a

Steele MacKaye, undated photo.
(Notable Names Database)

combination of his family's wealth, his own prodigious theatrical talent, and a knack for creating inventions. The family's wealth largely originated from his father, Colonel James MacKaye, who had served as a law clerk to Millard Fillmore before organizing a number of express companies, including Wells Fargo, and founding the American Telegraph Company, where he served as its president. While Colonel MacKaye's business success hinged on his legal and financial acumen, his son's was susceptible to the unpredictable highs and lows of pursuing a life in the arts.

As a young man, Steele had studied painting with William Hunt (brother of Richard, the architect of the Biltmore Estate and the Pinchot castle) and studied theater in France. At twenty-nine years old, he was packing American lecture halls with patrons who were eager to see MacKaye's revolutionary expressive acting technique ("a natural force in expression, as opposed to the artificial, over-emphatic style of the day"[12]). It was the beginning of a remarkable life in the public eye. In the two decades leading up to his World's Fair proposal, he had been the first American to play Hamlet in London, had patented more than one hundred inventions (including the folding theater seat, designed to speed evacuation in case of fire), had designed a theater with two elevator-operated stages that enabled forty-second scene changes, and had written and produced a spectacular show that brought Buffalo Bill Cody to Madison Square Garden. MacKaye also wrote some thirty plays, including his best received *Hazel Kirke*, which, with "a remarkable 486 performances," became the longest-running nonmusical play of its time.[13] (Interestingly, MacKaye wrote some of his plays in a cottage he rented near Bennington,

Vermont. It was the same cottage that Rudyard Kipling would rent with his family as they awaited the construction of their Vermont home.)[14]

As a youth, Steele MacKaye penned a phrase in his notebook that would resonate throughout his years: "We are never tired, so long as we can see far enough."[15] True to his mantra, he was always driving forward, his ideas often realized. One historian noted that "he had an amazing capacity for work, and a quality of inspiring others in enthusiasm for the work at hand. Two of his closest friends were Thomas Edison and Oscar Wilde. Edison said in a letter to MacKaye's son, "He was possessed of great imaginative power, together with an abnormal energy, ever seeking new worlds to conquer." It was Wilde who told him, "You and I can conquer the world, why not, let's do it."[16]

Thus, when MacKaye made his proposal to the commissioners of the World's Columbian Exposition of 1893, his reputation for achieving remarkable accomplishments gained him an immediate audience. MacKaye's vision was to create the largest theater the world had ever seen—a colossal edifice in every way, the building he dubbed "the Spectatorium" would literally place all of the great showman's accomplishments on the world stage in front of millions.

Daniel Burnham seized on the idea and at his bidding had Charles McKim draw up construction plans "that would combine the Spectatorium with the Terminal Station, a combined entrance structure to the fair. Early in the process there was too much competition for grounds within the fair proper, so MacKaye and his businessmen secured lake front property between fifty-sixth and fifty-seventh on Everett, covering an entire city block."[17]

The scale of MacKaye's vision was staggering, as was his need for success. What his potential partners may not have known was that while Steele MacKaye's triumphs and ingenuity had earned countless accolades, his lack of business acumen had left him practically penniless ("Business is the Heavy Villain of the play of life," he once lamented[18]). On September 30, 1891, he wrote a letter to his wife, referencing his dire circumstances and the possibilities his grand scheme could bring. After presenting a chart factoring in a salary of $600 per month and gross theater receipts of 10 percent, he said, "If the plan yields even one-third of this estimate, I shall earn enough, within the next two years, to make us independent for life, and can look forward to days of love, labor and well earned rest. I am struggling, with every prospect of success, to carry out this undertaking. Poor, almost penniless, as I am, it is a terrible strain. I have to appear a capitalist, with an empty purse in my pocket."[19]

Although he was no stranger to a feast-and-famine existence, MacKaye was weary of the uncertainty and stress of trying to hit on the next great success. He spent his days trying to rally support for the Spectatorium and trying to sell one of his plays, all the while acting as if all was fine. He asked his family to "try to eke it out a little longer," and said that he was heartsick with his inability to send relief. "Some fine day, not far off, we may wake up and find care banished for life. This hope sustains me," he wrote.[20]

The approval by the commissioners of the great fair was enough to lift MacKaye from despair and poverty—at least for a while. "Their hearty reception of my plans enabled me to arouse great interest in the enterprise," he reported.[21] In March 1892, the railroad industrialist George Pullman invested $50,000 in MacKaye's Spectatorium scheme, and others soon followed. In all, over $500,000 was raised to create the magnificent permanent structure on the shores of Lake Michigan.[22] The theater would be 480 feet long and 880 feet wide, with "an immense roof garden overlooking Jackson Park"; a seventeen-million-cubic-foot scenery department to provide "a startling advance in realism"; six miles of railroad track for moving scenery; a floodable stage floating life-size replicas of the *Pinta*, *Nina*, and *Santa Maria*; five-hundred-thousand-candlepower lighting; four-hundred-horsepower wind and wave machines; and seating for nine thousand patrons and standing room for an additional eight thousand.[23] MacKaye, who was writing a play commemorating Columbus's voyages to be featured in the theater, also commissioned composer Anton Dvorak* to write the primary score[24] (cellist/composer Victor Herbert would provide "pantomimic music"[25]).

But by April 1893, with the opening of the fair just weeks away and the gleaming city seemingly taunting him from across the street, Steele

---

*Dvorak's work would go on to be known as Symphony No. 9, "From the New World," which was first performed in New York City on December 15, 1893.

MacKaye was facing a perfect symphony of public and personal despair. A letter home told the tale:

> *The awful weather of the winter and the accidents caused by the wind have delayed the opening of the building until the 1st of July.—Meantime, if I don't raise $250,000 more within ten days, we shall be obliged to stop, and the greatest enterprise of this country will prove a fiasco.—I hate to write this, knowing you are already ill with care; but the time has come when I can no longer conceal it, and you may as well be prepared for the worst.* What I have been through no human being can ever imagine. *My will sustains me, and I am resigned to my fate.—I have sent you all my savings, and I shall send all I can, up to the last moment. Hoard for future possibilities. . . . Money is very hard to get. The whole country is on the verge of bankruptcy.*[26]

The financial panic of 1893, combined with the fact that millions of dollars were "locked up in hotels and special provisions for the World's Fair,"[27] helped speed the project toward failure. A *Chicago Times* article went on to say, "If the men who have grown rich upon MacKaye's ideas were to come forward now and put him on his feet, it would be but simple justice."[28] But nobody came forward, and despite a public plea for reason (an op-ed from MacKaye to the newspaper stating that the building was three-quarters completed, why not see it through?), the naysayers prevailed, and the Spectatorium was halted.

MacKaye sent for his three sons (Robert, Percy, and Benton, ages twenty-one, eighteen, and fourteen) to see the fair before it ended. One night, after the crowds had gone home, the MacKaye boys and their father gathered in the bright glow of the White City. Steele sat in his wheelchair, the one the boys had taken turns pushing as they traveled "along the magnificent distances of the Fair."[29] Nearby, one of the replica ships that had been built for Steele's magnificent production floated on Lake Michigan.

On Monday, September 25, 1893, Steele MacKaye took his three sons to see what they had dared not mention they wanted to see—the ruins of his life's greatest dream. As Percy MacKaye recalled,

My father, stricken in health, led my brothers and me, through cluttered debris, to an iron stairway that climbed steeply upward to nowhere.—Following his steps, silent, we ascended the dizzy height, overlooking the spacious plazas, fountains and domes of the Fair. Faintly the murmur of joyous humanity floated up to us where we stood on that edge of air. His eyes stared far off straight before him, dreamily, and his set jaw quivered. Then, for the first time, he spoke aloud:

"Boys, this is where it was to have been."

He spoke very simply. We looked in each other's eyes.—Then we descended, still silent.

"Was to have been": the words still burn.[30]

Steele MacKay would live but five months longer, done in by "the stress and strain of prolonged creative labour, the burden of vexatious financial questions, and finally the failure of the dearest object of his life."[31] He was fifty-one years old. The Spectatorium, for which MacKaye had raised close to a million dollars, to be built and reach three-quarters completion, was torn down and sold for scrap at a price of under $3,000.

Haunted and debilitated by the failure of his greatest dream, Steele MacKaye would die without ever knowing that one of his sons, who was present that day in Chicago and was deeply affected by his death, would go on to discover the restorative power of nature and become one of the most important visionaries in American conservation history.

CHAPTER FIVE

Passing the Baton

AFTER THE GREAT FAIR, OLMSTED TURNED MOST OF HIS ATTENTION TO the Biltmore project. At age seventy-three, however, it was clear that the estate would be the last remarkable showcase for his work. In the spring of 1895, he made the trip to Asheville, accompanied by his wife, Mary, and his daughter, Marion. Son Rick (Frederick Law Olmsted Jr.) was already apprenticing on the site and overseeing daily progress. During the visit, Rick noticed that his father was becoming increasingly forgetful. To avoid saying anything embarrassing in front of his client, Olmsted cut the trip short and returned home to Brookline, Massachusetts, with his wife and daughter.

Olmsted's dementia would accelerate over the next few years. In September 1898, he was admitted to the McLean Asylum outside Boston. Ironically, Olmsted had designed the grounds a quarter century before. In just under five years, he would be gone, but his remarkable designs—and, most important, his vision for them—would endure, in great measure because he left them in able hands.

Frederick Law Olmsted is fundamentally remembered and celebrated as an urban park planner. The hundreds of public spaces he designed and thousands of landscapes he influenced lay testament to this fact. But his imprint was greater still because he understood the transformative spiritual powers of nature and recognized when landscapes deserved to be left alone (as in the cases of Yosemite and Niagara Falls) or augmented with designs that minimized man-made structures to provide spaces for reflection and respite from daily burdens. In a January 1891 letter, he articulated the purpose of his designs, saying,

> *My notion is that whatever grounds a great city may need for other public purposes, for parades, for athletic sports, for fireworks, for museums of art or science such as botanic gardens, it also needs a large ground scientifically and artistically prepared to provide such a poetic and tranquilizing influence on its people as comes through a pleased contemplation of natural scenery, especially sequestered and limitless natural scenery.*[1]

Four years later, he would reflect on why an appreciation for scenery was the critical aspect of his craft. On the eve of receiving honors from Harvard University, he wrote, "The root of all of my good work is an early respect for, regard and enjoyment of scenery (the word tells much better of the fact than landscape) and extraordinary opportunities of cultivating susceptibility to the power of scenery. . . . Scenery to be looked upon contemplatively and which is provocative of musing moods."[2]

That he saw the need for such places before all but a handful of contemporaries did set the stage for new generations of conservationists to carry his mantle into the twentieth century and beyond.

A Profession Grows in the Biltmore Forest

Gifford Pinchot was seemingly always in a hurry. Practically from the time his father suggested a career in forestry, he set out on the mission to establish national forestry because it was "the one step most vitally needed to stop the forest butchery now so common and dangerous in the United States."[3] When afforded the opportunity to spend years in Europe immersing himself in the scientific and economic aspects of his profession, he chose to learn what he could in just over one year's time of intensive (mostly in the field) study, then headed back to America to get to work. As he reflected on that decision almost fifty years later, he said,

> *I intended to be a practicing forester all my life, yet I thought I could spare but thirteen months to get ready for my lifework. So I covered all*

the ground I could in the time I had for preparation. Today, with the long perspective behind me instead of ahead, I am still convinced my decision was right. A forester thoroughly trained in scientific forestry, if he had attempted to apply his knowledge to American forests in the early days, would have been doomed to fail.[4]

When Pinchot arrived back in America in 1890, he was more convinced than ever that his decision was on the mark, for, in his words, the country "was obsessed by a fury of development," in which only a small number of onlookers understood the consequences. Both the government and private landowners were felling trees at an extraordinary rate. Settlers and mining corporations were removing millions of board feet of timber from public lands yearly and not paying a cent for it. Pinchot lamented,

The American Colossus was fiercely intent on appropriating and exploiting the riches of the richest of all continents—grasping with both hands, reaping where he had not sown, wasting what he thought "would last forever." New railroads were opening new territory. The exploiters were pushing farther and farther into the wilderness. The man who could get his hands on the biggest slice of natural resources was the best citizen. Wealth and virtue were supposed to trot in double harness.[5]

At a time when not a single acre of federal land was managed as a working forest (and precious few state or private lands as well), Gifford Pinchot had entered the race against wholesale plundering, determined to have his management of the Biltmore Forest "prove what America did not yet understand, that trees could be cut and the forest preserved at one and the same time."[6]

He spent 1893 at the Biltmore Estate diligently working to do just that. In addition to managing and surveying Mr. Vanderbilt's expanding landholdings, he spent considerable time creating an exhibit for the Columbian Exposition in Chicago and a pamphlet to go along with it. From the start, Pinchot understood how important a role publicity would play in creating a forestry movement. Even so, he fretted about the amount of time he dedicated to the exhibit and the pamphlet and wondering if the state of North Carolina would pay their agreed-upon share.

By the end of the year, with the great fair project behind him and winter in the North Carolina mountains nigh, the restless Pinchot was able to throw all of his energy toward expanding his business and reputation. He opened an office in New York City and made it known that he was available for hire as a forestry consultant.

However, the affluent Amos R. Eno was not enthusiastic about his grandson's choice of profession. He offered Gifford a starting salary of $2,500 per year to work for him, plus the near certainty of attaining a fortune, but with his father's "strong approval," he turned the offer down.[7]

As many start-up businesses learn, there is often plenty of demand for free or cheap advice. This was true of Gifford Pinchot's enterprise as well, but in his optimistic fashion, he chose to look at it as being paid in experience. Nonetheless, he cleared $3,500 in year one (with no attendant promise of untold wealth attached, of course).[8] Even more important was that his work in 1894 began opening doors at the state and national level. Gifford Pinchot was getting noticed.

Chapter Six

Creating Fertile Ground

IN ECOLOGICAL TERMS, PIONEERING SPECIES ARE THOSE FIRST TO COLO-
nize a devastated landscape, creating conditions for subsequent arrivals—
typically seeds blown in by the wind or dropped by birds or wandering
mammals—to take root and thrive. Similarly, Gifford Pinchot's national
forestry initiative would probably have failed to take root unless a few
pioneers had prepared the soil for him in advance.

George Perkins Marsh, whose
book *Man and Nature* had so
impacted James Pinchot, and by
extension his son, was one of the
first to sow his ideas upon the barren
landscape. Another important early
contributor who was influenced by
Marsh was an Upstate New Yorker
named Franklin B. Hough.

Born July 20, 1822, Franklin
Benjamin Hough was the son of
the first medical doctor to reside
in Lewis County, New York. As
a youngster, Franklin enjoyed
exploring the nearby woods and
collecting rocks, one of his many
lifelong pursuits. After graduating from Union College in 1843,

Franklin Benjamin Hough, circa
1880–1885. (Library of Congress)

39

Hough attended Cleveland Medical College, where he received his MD. Yet, within a few years, his role as a practicing physician was being subsumed by his many other hobbies, and "the life of a doctor [seemed] always to have been a sideline."[1]

Like Olmsted, Hough was a man of many interests. Botany, geology, mineralogy, and meteorology were all important to his self-education and soon eclipsed his medical practice because he was making his mark as a local historian and writer. Just four years after receiving his degree from Cleveland Medical College, he ceased practicing medicine to devote his time to research and writing. By 1855, his published accounts of the histories of New York counties had gained him enough notoriety to become appointed as the superintendent of the New York State Census for 1855 and 1865.[2] During the Civil War, he briefly joined the U.S. Sanitary Commission, where he likely crossed paths with Executive Secretary Frederick Law Olmsted.

Hough probably would have been content focusing on his writing career—he would author or contribute to over three hundred pieces—but when he read *Man and Nature* in 1864, his professional life changed forever. Marsh's case for forest conservation hit home with the man who had witnessed how "the vast primeval forests of the Adirondack wilderness were gradually thinned out as the lumbering, leather tanning, and iron industries took the best timber for their needs"[3] and then moved on. By 1872, influenced by reports of devastation left in the wake of lumbering operations, the state of New York's legislature appointed a commission to survey the Adirondack region and recommend courses of action. Hough was named to that commission (as was the conservationist and future publisher of *Garden and Forest* magazine Charles Sprague Sargent). Although the commission's recommendations were not embraced, Hough continued banging the drum for forest restoration.

One year later, Hough presented a paper titled "On the Duty of Governments in the Preservation of Forests" at the meeting of the American Association for the Advancement of Science in Portland, Maine. By now, his conviction to preserve forests as manageable assets was well established. In addition to mitigating the effects of floods and droughts, he stated that *the economic value of timber, and our absolute dependence upon it for innumerable uses in manufactures and the arts, the rapidly increasing demand for it in railroad construction and the positive necessity for its use in the affairs of common life, even were its use as fuel largely supplanted by the introduction of mineral coal, are too obvious for suggestion.*[4]

The needs for well-managed forests, Hough argued, were clear. But how could we ensure that the forests so vital to mitigating natural disasters and contributing to America's economic strength would become a national priority? By immediately embracing two initiatives: the regulation of forests and the establishment of forestry schools.

Hough's presentation was so well received that the association established a committee to educate state legislatures and Congress about the dangers of deforestation. (Hough was subsequently named chairman.)

As was the case when Olmsted was named superintendent of Central Park, Hough had navigated toward a role he was ready-made (and self-made) to assume. His scientific bearing, love of nature, ability to communicate, and willingness to travel throughout the country (and the world) in the name of formally establishing forests and forestry practices inspired others to join the cause.

Within three years, his committee's lobbying efforts succeeded. In 1876, Congress determined that a federal assessment of the state of forests and lumber was warranted and created the office of special agent in the Department of Agriculture to take on the task. Once again, Franklin B. Hough was called upon to lead the charge. And again, he was prepared.

Hough compiled the data and observations he'd made over the preceding five years into a compendium he titled *Report upon Forestry*. It is fair to say that Congress had not to date received such a comprehensive assessment. Its 650 pages predictably stated the case for new forestry practices (citing wasteful uses of lands and the "useless destruction of our forests"[5] caused by lumber interests claiming to be homesteaders, among other egregious acts) and the potential economic benefits of addressing the misuse of lands and creating managed forest preserves. The thoroughness of Hough's report was impressive, covering everything from proper seed gathering, preservation, and planting techniques to the establishment of forestry schools modeled after those in Europe, including suggested curriculum.

Hough's report (and those to follow) "laid a solid foundation for serious discussion of American forest conditions at the height of the Industrial Revolution"[6] and, importantly, advocated for forests to be working, productive entities (as opposed to "the 'forever wild' concept of an unproductive forest park"[7]). By 1881, Hough reached the apex of his career when the U.S. Division of Forestry was established and he was named its first chief, a position he would hold for two years. (In a most controversial move, Hough was demoted by agricultural commissioner George P. Loring and replaced by Nathaniel Egleston, "a political appointee with little forestry knowledge."[8] To contemporary observers, the demotion of Hough, a man so identified with the cause of national forestry, in favor of a clergyman-teacher best known for his essays about planting ornamental trees in urban landscapes "seemed petty, personal and political."[9])

Egleston's tenure would only last three years. Comparisons to Hough's accomplishments were likely inevitable, but even without them, it was obvious Egleston wasn't up to the task. Gifford Pinchot's assessment of Egleston's contribution to American forestry warranted a few scathing lines:

> *Dr. N. H. Egleston [was] one of those failures in life whom the spoils of the system is constantly catapulting into responsible positions. . . . After three years of innocuous desuetude, Dr. Egleston in turn was replaced.*[10]

It was Egleston's replacement, Dr. Bernhard Fernow, who would offer Gifford Pinchot his first federal job as assistant chief of the Forestry Division with an opportunity for advancement. Ultimately, Pinchot would turn down the job (despite having already accepted it) in part because of the strong advice of Charles Sprague Sargent, whose counsel the young forester respected. Two situations helped convince Pinchot that Sargent was right. The first was a trip with Fernow to survey the forests of Arkansas, during which "the first indications of a basic personality clash between the two men developed."[11] The second was the opportunity to manage the Biltmore Forest.

When Pinchot wrote to formally decline the position Fernow had held for him, the head of the Forestry Division was rightfully miffed. But they were not good candidates for a durable partnership. As historian M. Nelson McGeary noted, "Their conceptions of forestry were so different . . . and their personalities collided so forcibly that each lost respect for the activities of the other. Pinchot was impatient to accomplish things in a hurry; Fernow was in favor of moving more gradually. Jealousy undoubtedly contributed to their attitudes."[12]

In the end, they would both be credited with moving the cause of American forestry forward. At the very least, Fernow was the first professionally trained forester to lead the agency.

CHAPTER SEVEN

Making the Push

GIFFORD PINCHOT BELIEVED THAT THE FUTURE OF FORESTRY AS A profession could only be secured by making strong political alliances and by showing America's citizens how sustainable forestry practices were vital to their economic, physical, and mental well-being. The backing of the general citizenry would be critical, for public opinion had the power to sway politicians who otherwise would have been beholden to the monied few. To be certain, despite the efforts of George Perkins Marsh, Franklin Hough, and others, forestry still needed an evangelist to show the way.

Pinchot understood that one choice was to "urge, beg and implore: to preach at, call upon, and beseech the American people to stop forest destruction and practice Forestry; and denounce them if they didn't"[1]— something he felt that the few existing forestry associations and other advocates for forested lands had been doing for more than two decades with no professionally managed forests to show for it.

It was better, he believed, to "choose action instead of exhortation," to demonstrate sustainable practices in action, to prove the many advantages of managing forested lands and therefore sway public opinion. The pragmatic Pinchot felt that he'd be going it alone (his autobiography was titled *Breaking New Ground* for a reason, after all). He couldn't side with strict forest preservationists, those who felt that the only way to save forests was to leave them completely alone. That course wasn't consistent with Pinchot's beliefs. Nor could he side with "the lumberman, because forest destruction was their daily bread."[2]

"The job was not to stop the ax, but to regulate its use," he wrote. "For that the whole stream of public thinking about the forest had to be shifted into a new channel. . . . A nation utterly absorbed in the present had to be brought to consider the future. The ingrained habit of mind of the best part of a hundred million people about a fundamental necessity of human life had to be changed."[3]

He felt that he stood at the beginning of an interminably long trail that he would be blazing alone. He often stated as much as if it were fact. More accurately, it was "an embroidery of the truth." A handful of others had prepared the ground, and Gifford Pinchot was about to benefit from their efforts to become the most visible leader of a movement. Joined and enabled by like-minded writers, artists, and politicians, he would guide the next phase of conservation history—a tremendous accomplishment for which he deserved most but not all of the credit.

GARDEN AND FOREST

Pinchot's feeling that he was going it alone was a persistent narrative theme that was largely based on facts. Since his days at Yale, when he discovered that there really was no professional path forward for a budding American forester and he would need to go to Europe to further his quest, he felt the need to establish himself as the pioneer in his field (and as we have seen, he was in a hurry to do so). But the truth was he couldn't rise up without the help of others.

It was the support of his parents that steered him toward forestry in the first place, financed his education at Yale and in Europe, and provided emotional support when Gifford questioned whether he should continue his career or take the opportunity his grandfather Amos had placed in front of him.

The most able foresters in the world, Dr. Dietrich Brandis ("the first of the living foresters"[4]) and assistant director of the L'Ecole Nationale Forestiere, Professor Lucien Boppe, had treated Gifford Pinchot as their protégé, encouraging him to ply their trade in America, despite the odds.

The Dodge and Phelps Company hired Gifford (for the cost of travel and lodging expenses) to survey their lands and give his fledgling career a sense of credibility. And, most notably, Frederick Law Olmsted propelled his career onto the national stage when he called on young Gifford to implement the forestry plan for the Biltmore Forest.

Pinchot acknowledged the impact Olmsted had on his career by saying,

> *What was worth almost more than the opportunity to work was the fact that Mr. Olmsted took my profession seriously, and took with equal seriousness the assumption which he made that I was able to practice it. I have never forgotten what it meant to a youngster just getting started to be treated to some extent as an equal, and I shall always hold myself deep in his debt for what he did for me.*[5]

What Pinchot may never have known is that Olmsted had a hand in another enterprise that helped ensure that the profession of forestry would become a national concern—*Garden and Forest* magazine.

In 1888, the first issue of *Garden and Forest* was published—a vision that came to fruition through the significant contributions of Olmsted, who sent a check for $500 and provided advice on both the content and the contributors over the three years leading up to its debut.[6]

Founded by Charles Sprague Sargent, who had been named the first director of Harvard University's Arnold Arboretum at age thirty-one, and edited by William A. Stiles, a highly regarded editorial writer for the *New York Tribune*, the magazine was a voice for conservation unlike any publication of its time. Indeed, one historian notes that *Garden and Forest*

> *sought nothing less than to redefine the relation of people to the natural world in a bold, new way. It brought the attention to thousands of wild and domesticated plant species, shaped several new environmental professions, defended various urban, state and national parks, spurred the establishment of many forest reserves, and created a powerful voice for reform.*[7]

And voice for reform it was. Inspired by the works of George Perkins Marsh (whom Sargent credited with kindling his interest in forests and

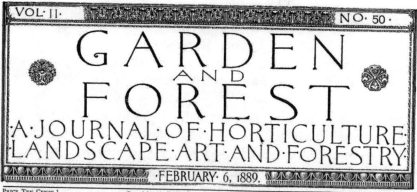

VOL· II·   NO· 50·

GARDEN AND FOREST

·A·JOURNAL·OF·HORTICULTURE· ·LANDSCAPE·ART·AND·FORESTRY·

·FEBRUARY· 6, 1889·

PRICE TEN CENTS.]   Copyright, 1889, by THE GARDEN AND FOREST PUBLISHING COMPANY.   [$4.00 A YEAR, IN ADVANCE.

Garden and Forest magazine advertising page of 1889. (Library of Congress) forest preservation) and Olmsted (whose views on the importance of natural settings to spiritual, mental, and physical health were of particular interest to Stiles), *Garden and Forest* featured the work of an impressive range of contributors. Botanists, foresters, horticulturalists, journalists, and artists were frequently featured, with writers such as John Muir and Edward Everett Hale (author of *The Man without a Country*) setting the publication's standard for writing excellence with a distinct point of view. The need to retain natural places (in both urban and rural environments) for the benefit of all, not "sacrificed for the sake of material development or monopolized by the few,"[8] was one of the foundational messages of the magazine from day one.

In 1890, when Gifford Pinchot was studying forestry in France, he already knew that he would need help to make his new profession a national priority. Friends and business acquaintances would surely help, but he would also need to sway public opinion. Thus, before he was even back in America, he was already writing for *Garden and Forest*. In a July 1890 article titled "The Sihlwald.—1," he wrote, "So often lost sight of [is the fact] that the protection of forests is not an end, but a means, and that the whole question of forestry has a very definite and important financial bearing."[9] Not yet twenty-five years old, the budding forester already knew that establishing the economic value of forests in the public's mind would be vital to his success. And he knew just where to go to get the word out.

Sargent and Stiles would turn up a few times along Pinchot's career path. Two days after his return from school in France, Pinchot sought out Stiles in New York City, whom he described as "a slow-spoken emaciated Jerseyman, a politician turned philanthropist, with uncommon knowledge of what American Forestry should mean, and where it ought to be headed."[10]

On the other hand, Sargent, with whom Pinchot visited a few days later, was "generally glum," warning the young forester not to accept Dr. Fernow's offer to work with him in the Forestry Division and wondering aloud whether either he or Gifford would live to see "a practical system of forest control" in America. But at least Pinchot left the meeting knowing that his articles making cogent, impassioned arguments for the creation of American forest reserves and their management would continue to appear in front of a receptive, influential audience of *Garden and Forest* readers.

The two-pronged approach of becoming a practicing forest manager and generating public awareness of the need for forestry to be regulated in the interest of safety and enduring economic security made Pinchot's ascent as a public figure possible. And in 1894, he was on the verge of an important move.

CHAPTER EIGHT

Benton Finds His Way

IN 1894, AS GIFFORD PINCHOT WAS EMBARKING ON HIS CAREER AS A forestry consultant, a fourteen-year-old boy in Massachusetts was sorting through the pieces of a family crisis. The death of Benton MacKaye's father, Steele, in February of that year left him hurt and bewildered.

Just four years prior, young Benton had spent the winter and spring in Washington, DC, with his mother, his sister Hazel, and his Aunt Sadie in a boarding house. (Brother Percy moved in with siblings Harold and James, who already had steady government jobs, which was the reason for the family's visit—Steele's most recent play had been a flop, and the family needed to achieve a semblance of financial stability.)

But Benton found his time in DC exhilarating. One highlight was attending a lecture by the Civil War hero John Wesley Powell, who regaled the over seven hundred in attendance with tales of his 1869 expedition down the Colorado River. Benton was enthralled and bitten by the expedition bug (he would subsequently hear Robert E. Peary speak of his upcoming maiden Arctic voyage).[1] The MacKayes moved in affluent circles due to the renown of Benton's grandfather and father, and doors continued to open for the inquisitive youngster, despite his shy demeanor.

Several days a week, he was allowed to visit the Smithsonian Institution. He brought a tripod camp stool and sketch pad with him and sat for hours rendering copies of his favorite paintings. It wasn't long before the curators invited him into the back rooms, where he could sketch items from the collection at his leisure. His favorite things to draw were birds, mollusks, and other artifacts that had been donated but weren't on display.

But for Steele MacKaye and family, affluence was more appearance than fact. While the public witnessed the theater-packing success of his most famous work, *Hazel Kirke*, the family didn't, for Steele had signed away the rights of his play to the promoters. And even when the money rolled in, such as when Steele MacKaye brought Buffalo Bill Cody to Madison Square Garden, it was never long enough to outlast his next great idea.

In 1887, after living through eight years of Steele MacKaye's poor business decisions and his eternal promises of being on the verge of a financial breakthrough—years in which the family had bounced between farmhouses in Vermont, Massachusetts, New York, and Connecticut—Benton's older brother, William, was able to purchase a farmhouse in Shirley, Massachusetts, where the family could settle and reestablish themselves.

It took less than six months for the MacKayes to find out just how fortuitous William's purchase was. On April 8, 1888, Benton's grandfather, Colonel James MacKaye (who had been in on the founding of Wells Fargo and the American Telegraph Company and had subsequently amassed great wealth), passed away in Paris. He bequeathed most of his fortune to his half-brother, William ("doubtless with the expectation that, having no children, he would pass it on to Steele MacKaye and his children," reported Benton's older brother, Percy[2]).

A few days later, William told Steele's wife, Mary, that he had drawn up a will that would leave everything to his wife in the event of his death (William and his wife, Maggie, had no children). Miraculously, the next day, William died of a stroke. Even more incredibly, his wife Maggie died less than a month later, "from no other illness than her extreme grief."[3] Thus, in less than six weeks, the MacKaye family fortune was no longer even the MacKayes'. It is small wonder that Steele MacKaye's drive to regain the family's status had motivated him so powerfully and desperately to bring his Spectatorium to fruition.

And now, in the late winter of 1894, not quite yet fifteen-year-old Benton MacKaye was facing the harshest of realities. There would be no more majestic schemes to propel them back into affluence. It seemed as if Steele MacKaye's words "was to have been" had become the family motto. Benton became so despondent that he briefly contemplated suicide, but decided better of it, perhaps buoyed somewhat by his daily walks and explorations of the hills and streams surrounding the MacKaye cottage, which began the year before.

Benton described his first springtime walks in 1893 "as a release from jail after a winter cooped up in New York." Indeed, his early walks inspired him to explore the rural Massachusetts countryside surrounding the cottage. In a book released in honor of his ninetieth birthday, he reflected on the importance of those jaunts.

> *I would explore the country within walking distance of my home in Shirley Center (radius four miles). I would in particular map the forest, "deciduous and evergreen" (my first stunt in forestry). And in general I'd scan the region's habitability (my first stunt in geotechnics). I would number my expeditions: "No. 1," "No. 2," "No. 3," etc. And off I went.*[4]

The MacKaye homestead and surroundings thus became Benton's touchstones—places where he could explore forests, hillsides, and ideas in relative solitude. The places that would shape his career in forestry, his advocacy for conservation, and his understanding of the restorative qualities of nature. All three would emerge on the American stage in the decades to come. What he couldn't know is that Gifford Pinchot was laying the groundwork for him to succeed.

CHAPTER NINE

Facing the Headwinds of Change

TURNING DOWN FORESTRY DIVISION CHIEF FERNOW'S OFFER TO TAKE a federal post meant that Pinchot would need to find another route to implement his vision for forestry on a national scale. Fortunately, another mentor, Charles Sprague Sargent, was still in his corner. (It was Sargent who had advised Pinchot not to work with Fernow in the first place and had been supportive of Pinchot's efforts to make forest protection a national priority.) But the barriers to change were formidable and seemingly intractable. The unregulated state of public lands fostered a feeling that "whoever got there first could enjoy the spoils," and frankly most politicians didn't understand or care to look to discover any downside to the status quo.

Thus, during the last twenty-five years of the nineteenth century, various legislative attempts to halt the destruction of public timberlands were introduced, but few gained traction. One of the most interesting proposals was drafted in 1888 by Fernow himself, then chief of the U.S. Division of Forestry. Presented to Congress by the American Forestry Association, the bill called for four men to "inspect personally all the forested lands at least once every year" and authorized the president "to employ the land and naval forces of the United States for the protection of forest lands," ideas Pinchot found unusual, unenforceable, and "like so much of the forest legislation proposed about this time . . . based on an amazing ignorance of actual conditions in the West."[1] But, Pinchot conceded, there was one good idea contained in Fernow's proposal: the ability for the president to create forest reservations by executive order.

As the 1880s ended, those who cared most about America's forests felt as if the need to address the problem was exceeded only by Congress's inability to take it on. The consequences of doing nothing were laid bare by former secretary of the interior Carl Schurz in a speech to the American Forestry Association and the Pennsylvania Forestry Association when he said, "The more study and thought I have given the matter, the firmer has become my conviction that the destruction of the forests of this country will be the murder of its future prosperity and progress."[2] Schurz then listed those he felt were complicit in the act: timber thieves (who were "stealing whole forests"—enough to keep sawmills running at full capacity and filling the pockets of robbers at the expense of the American public"[3]), campers, settlers, miners, the general public, and the government itself. "It is public opinion looking with indifference on this wanton, barbarous, disgraceful vandalism," he said. "It is a spendthrift people recklessly wasting its heritage. It is a government careless of the future and unmindful of a pressing duty."[4]

Schurz's frustration had been simmering since he was unable to halt the plundering of the forests when he headed the Interior Department in the preceding decade. He decried that he had little power to address "the commercial depredations upon the property of the people," and that his attempts to take action had been met with telegrams of protest from "regions most concerned," members of Congress "with wrath in their eyes," and commentary deriding his German heritage.[5]

The conclusion of Schurz's 1889 speech to forestry associations made the strongest possible case that America's resources were not inexhaustible and that we could not continue to live as if there were no tomorrow.

I regret, we cannot forcibly enough impress upon the American people the necessity of speedy measures looking to the preservation of our mountain forests which, when once destroyed, cannot be renewed. Unless this can be done in time, our children will curse the almost criminal improvidence of their ancestors, but if it is done in time, those who are instrumental in doing it will deserve and will have the blessings of future generations. . . . It is the cowardice of the small politician who, instead of studying the best interests of the people, trembles

*lest doing his full duty may cost him a vote and who is not seldom apt
to fear the resentment of thieves more than that of honest men.*[6]

Seventeen months after Schurz's speech, the decades-long pleas for forestry reform from the citizenry, trade organizations, botanists, and foresters finally inspired congressional action. Introduced by Secretary John Noble of the Department of the Interior and Edward Bowers of the General Land Office, the Noble-Bowers Amendment, signed into law on March 3, 1891, gave the president authority to establish forest reserves from existing publicly held land. Hailed by Pinchot as "the most important legislation in the history of Forestry in America,"[7] it would be evoked by President Benjamin Harrison to set aside thirteen million acres of land as forest reserves during his presidency alone.

Formally establishing forest reserves was unquestionably an important step. But from at least one forester's point of view, the law's dictates were too severe. In his autobiography, Pinchot lamented that "under [the law] no timber could be cut, no forage could be grazed, no minerals could be mined, nor any road built in any Forest Reserve."[8]

What's more, Pinchot pointed out, the new law did nothing to address the problem of resources being stolen from public lands because the penalties were "practically unknown" and there were no resources for enforcing them. As far as Pinchot was concerned, the legislation's greatest contribution to forestry was that the president had the power to create reserves. To ensure that those reserves were managed for the benefit of both the forest and the public would be his next great challenge.

CHAPTER TEN

The Adirondacks Stir Debate

IN HIS 1882 ANNUAL STATE ADDRESS, NEW YORK GOVERNOR ALONZO B. Cornell touched on various subjects—transportation, tourism, and the like, as was typical for such speeches. But one subject could not be covered in a few sentences. The state had acquired hundreds of thousands of acres of land in the Adirondack region because private parties had purchased the properties from the state at nominal prices, "cut off the marketable timber where accessible, then abandoned to the State the clearings, [now] worthless generally for Agricultural purposes; thereby escaping the payment of taxes."[1] The situation caused the governor to question the state's policy of selling the land they had acquired due to nonpayment of taxes, or would in the future. "It might be leased, perhaps ... for certain purposes; but its uses should be carefully restricted," he offered, for if "the Adirondack region ... the natural and principal watershed of important navigable waters [is] divested of its timber, imminent danger will threaten."[2]

Not long after Cornell's speech, the New York legislature established a Commission on State Parks to review the state's landholdings and make recommendations. Not surprisingly, native son Franklin Benjamin Hough was named to the commission (although this time, he would not be its chairperson).

The decade of inaction on the recommendations submitted by the 1872 Commission on State Parks had left the region, and the state, facing lingering economic uncertainty that had simply grown to the point where something needed to be done. The first commission's call to preserve the Adirondack region's forest in their report of 1873 had nothing to do with recreation. Their concern was that the damage done by "cut and run" foresters would devastate New York's businesses that depended on navigable rivers and canals to power their factories and to bring their goods to market. The destruction to the springs and streams that hindered the flow of the Hudson River, the Erie Canal, and other navigable waters would also threaten the livelihoods of farmers. Stripping the land also brought the incessant threat of fires and floods.[3]

When forests were cleared, boughs, treetops, wood chips, and small branches littered the landscape. Once dried, a lightning bolt, campfire, or the sparks from a passing train were all it took to start a disastrous inferno, threatening lives and livelihoods and leaving yet another hazard in its wake, that of flash floods.

Hough's commission believed that the only solution was state intervention. Their report succinctly stated that, "when we find individuals managing their property in a reckless and selfish manner, without regard for the vested rights of others, it becomes the duty of the State to interfere and provide a remedy. Here, by ruthless destruction of the forest, thoughtless men are depriving the country of a water supply which has belonged to it from time immemorial, and the public interest demands legislative protection."[4]

Because the legislature had done little in the interceding nine years before Cornell made his address, the state had continued accumulating the land that was left in default by cut-and-run landowners. Eventually New York would own more than seven hundred thousand acres of clear-cut land in the Adirondack region.[5] Loggers, with a twenty-five-year crop cycle, had no incentive but to fell trees, make money, and move on to a new parcel, where the cycle would begin anew.

By the mid-1850s, the ongoing threats to the environment and commerce left in the wake of indiscriminate logging had the effect of forging new coalitions that desperately wanted the practice either regulated or halted completely. Merchants who relied on the Erie Canal, the operators of the canal, and the chamber of commerce wanted to ensure that the canal remained a viable competitor to the railroads to help keep shipping costs competitive. One prerequisite was a canal provided with steadily flowing water, which could not be guaranteed if the Adirondack forests were laid to waste. These influential business leaders "had no particular interest, one way or the other, in how the state used or did not use its forests; their interest was in maintaining a streamflow which, they were convinced, was linked to forest preservation."[6]

In addition to the merchants and canal supporters, the coalition to save the Adirondacks from saws and axes included those who had built estates in the region, businesses that relied on tourism, and various hiking, fishing, and hunting clubs that were forming and buying tracts in the area where they could host members and guests.

One option available to the state—one that would have addressed the concerns of those opposed to clear-cutting and additionally would have provided the state with sustained revenue—was to professionally manage the Adirondack forests. The fact that conservation did not carry the day, "despite the potential and actual constituency for conservation—merchants, foresters, lumberers and taxpayers—[indicated] a quite extraordinary effort on the part of preservationists, for whom an alternate, more expensive solution was attractive."[7]

But the damage done by the cut-and-run woodlot owners was too great to overcome. Newspapers covering the destruction of the Adirondacks "insisted that the lumberman, almost without exception, was a ruthless, arrogant, greedy destroyer of the bounty of nature."[8] Faced with overwhelming opposition, advocates for scientific forestry found it difficult to be heard. In the Adirondacks at least, poor forestry practices had become the standard by which all foresters were judged—an activity "that threatened to destroy both recreation and commerce."[9]

On May 20, 1892, New York state governor Roswell P. Flower signed the law creating a 2.8-million-acre Adirondack Park. To Gifford Pinchot, who had lobbied for scientific forestry to be practiced in the Adirondack Preserve, it was a harsh defeat he would never forget. More than fifty years after the creation of the Adirondack State Forest Preserve, he wrote, "The exclusion of Forestry from the Preserve was made certain, in 1891, by an amendment to the State Constitution which forbade the cutting of any tree. That indefensible provision is still in force."[10]

To preservationists, the protection of the Adirondacks was an early and important victory in their efforts to ensure that some of America's lands remained "forever wild."

CHAPTER ELEVEN

A Forester without Forests

IN 1889, AS THE ISSUES CONCERNING THE ADIRONDACK PRESERVE's creation, protection, and management were being articulated, debated, and put forth to the public, an editorial appeared in *Garden and Forest* urging immediate action to protect federal forest-bearing lands. In it, editor Charles Sargent called for a temporary halt "from sale or entry; temporary use of the Army to protect them; and the appointment by the President of a commission to report to Congress a plan of administration and control."[1]

While the plan was embraced by the American Forestry Association and received a lot of press, it hardly gained traction. As Pinchot noted, halting land sales was politically impossible and the training of army officers to be "an enlisted body of forest guards" wouldn't rise to the level of training required to manage forests. But the third part of Sargent's plan, the formation of a commission to study and recommend a federal plan for managing forests, was "a long shot into the bull's eye," said Pinchot, "and for it, Sargent deserves immense credit, in spite of what came after."[2]

"What came after" would eventually cost Pinchot another mentor and friendship, but their common bond of urging the protection of federal lands was enough to hold their alliance together for the next seven years.

In December 1894, Sargent called a meeting attended by his coeditor Stiles, Pinchot, and Robert Underwood Johnson, editor of *Century* magazine. Frustrated by the inactivity of Congress, they agreed it was time to do something about the lack of permanent policies concerning national forests. The group created an outline for a bill that would authorize the president to appoint a commission to study public timber holdings and present recommendations for how they should be managed. The New York Chamber of Commerce quickly passed a resolution endorsing the idea and sent a copy of the nascent bill's outline to every member of Congress, where momentum was stymied again ("the usual result—nothing," Pinchot noted).[3]

The methodical Sargent and impatient Pinchot would seem unlikely partners, but both were completely dedicated to the cause of creating national forests. Sargent's magazine and Pinchot's willingness to lecture to political and trade organizations to build support were apt to take hold if only they could find the right formula for getting it done.

On June 5, 1895, after more than six years of trying, they broke through. This time it was Pinchot who called the meeting where a new initiative would take root. He, Sargent, and Stiles met Dr. Wolcott Gibbs, president and founder of the National Academy of Sciences, at Sargent's home in Brookline, Massachusetts. Notable for his achievements in analytical and inorganic chemistry, Gibbs was also deeply committed to conservation. (Interestingly, his past experiences also included working with Frederick Law Olmsted on the Sanitary Commission during the Civil War, and with whom he cofounded the Union League Club in 1863.) Pinchot had gotten wind that Gibbs was particularly "appalled at the wanton exploitation of the nation's forest and mineral lands that was occurring as a result of the activities of the lumber and mining companies" and was ready to share a suggestion for reining them in.[4]

The National Academy of Sciences, established by an act of Congress and signed into law by Abraham Lincoln in 1863, was created to provide objective advice to the nation as requested by government agencies and departments. Gibbs suggested enlisting the secretary of the interior, Hoke Smith, to officially request a National Academy commission to study how to protect America's timberlands from fire while sustaining tree harvests; the effect of forests on soil, climate, and water conditions; and what legislation should be enacted or revised to support the commission's findings. No one was more enthusiastic about the plan than Pinchot, who noted that "a National Academy Commission would be made up of [scientists] with free and open minds, not of politicians with political debts to constituents determined to keep on with their looting."[5]

In February 1896, the members of the National Forest Commission were named. Six, including Sargent, who was named chairman, were members of the National Academy of Sciences and represented a variety of disciplines including stream hydrology, geology, zoology, and forestry. The seventh member, who would later be elected secretary of the commission, was Gifford Pinchot.

It didn't take long for Sargent's and Pinchot's differences in style and opinions to emerge. Pinchot urged the commission to make haste because they had less than a year to get anything signed by President Cleveland before he left office in March 1897. At the first meeting in April 1896, Pinchot and committee member Arnold Hague (a geologist and explorer with a knowledge of western forests and significant Washington connections) were assigned the task of delivering a preliminary report and recommendations at the May meeting in three weeks.

Pinchot was already aware that President Cleveland was on the side of forestry. In his first address as president, he stated that "the time has come when efficient measures should be taken for the preservation of our forests from indiscriminate and remediless destruction."[6] In a meeting with Arnold Hague, the chief executive expressed that he hoped that some of the committee's findings could be worked into his November address to Congress so there would be hope of enacting legislation before he left office.

He also made four recommendations directly to the National Forest Commission:

1. Develop a plan for organizing a forest service before considering the addition of more forest reserves.

2. Create a plan that looks small and costs little to make it most appealing to Congress.

3. Create a plan that minimizes controversy and "reaches its object, if possible, along other lines."

4. Prepare the bills necessary to carry out the plan with the cooperation of "someone thoroughly familiar with the temper of Congress."[7]

Despite this clear directive, Sargent was in no hurry to keep the commission's project on track, advising Pinchot, "My whole idea is to go slow and feel our way—not to attempt too much, and take plenty of time."[8] Further, his autocratic style and outright opposition to Cleveland's plan or even to consider "the forest problem" from a forester's point of view infuriated Pinchot. Concerned that the inventory of western forests would not be done in time to meet Cleveland's schedule, Pinchot enlisted old Yale classmate and fellow forester Henry Graves (whom Pinchot referred to by his college nickname "Harry") to head out west two months before the committee was scheduled to begin their tour.

It wasn't only the pace of information gathering that bothered Pinchot. Sargent wasn't backing down from his position that army soldiers should guard the perimeter of national forests and be trained to become foresters. Conversely, Pinchot believed that the lands should be managed by professional foresters who would also be granted the authority to enforce applicable laws. Pinchot was careful not to question Sargent's views in public, particularly because he admired his achievements, including his roles as the director of the Arnold Arboretum, cofounder of *Gardens and Forests*, and tireless advocate for public lands. But Sargent was a botanist, not a forester, which automatically diminished his understanding of what was required in Pinchot's view.

When Graves and Pinchot met fellow commission members Sargent, Hague, Yale professor of botany William H. Brewer, and retired U.S. Army Corps general Henry L. Abbott in Montana on July 16, 1896, they also had a special guest in tow. His name was John Muir. It was the first time he and Pinchot had met, which the forester said was a "great delight," then added that Muir was "a most fascinating talker. I took to him at once."[9] Muir stayed with the group as they explored the Bitterroot Valley, made their way to Klamath Lake and Crater Lake in Oregon, went south to California's Sierra Nevada Mountains, then east to the Grand Canyon. While the others took a side trip, Pinchot and Muir spent one day plus camping on the rim of the magnificent canyon. ("When we came across a tarantula, he wouldn't let me kill it. He said it had as much right there as we did," said Pinchot.[10])

President Cleveland wanted the commission's administrative plan for the country's forest reserves on his desk by November 1, 1896. At the beginning of October, David R. Francis (who had replaced Hoke Smith as secretary of the interior) asked for a report as well so that he could incorporate the committee's recommendations into his annual report.

More than three weeks passed before the committee met to discuss courses of action. The only thing they could agree on was creating new reserves. Sargent was adamant about not presenting a plan for managing the forests and not proposing legislation in the upcoming session of Congress. Pinchot pointed out that to create reserves without any plan for managing them would create the misconception that the forests would "be taken out of circulation and locked up." He believed that Congress and the people who would be most affected by the creation of new reserves—ranchers, foresters, and neighboring communities—were entitled to know that management, not preservation, was the committee's intent. "The Commission's refusal to make such a statement was a blunder of the first water. What made it all the worse was that strong Western sentiment could have been brought to the support of the Reserves if we had tried to arouse it," he said.[11]

The only positive development to come out of the last (and only fully attended) meeting of the National Forest Commission was the decision to recommend new forest reserves to the president in time for them to be created. The thirteen forest reserves in seven states that President Cleveland created by executive order on February 22, 1897 (just ten days before he would leave office), more than doubled the size of those lands from 17.5 million to almost 39 million acres.

But that was the only good news, for the reaction to the new reserves was disastrous. Pinchot blamed the uproar entirely on Sargent's incompetence. The commission had been given simple marching orders and a timetable for getting them done, and Sargent had stood in the way. The commission's work was also conducted largely in secret at Sargent's behest. The failure to build consensus or to conduct any form of outreach was a lost opportunity and contributed to the uproar that followed. Pinchot wrote,

If the Commission had reported its plan for managing the Reserves at the time it recommended the new Reserves, how many Senators and Congressmen who were driven into bitter and lasting hostility would have been friendly, because they would have had no excuse to be otherwise? How many newspapers, associations, interests, would have been with us, or at least not against us, who can tell? How many millions of acres now denuded would be green with growing trees? The whole forest movement paid dearly for Sargent's contrariness, however sound to him the reasons that lay back of it.[12]

The hardest part for Pinchot to swallow was that the National Forest Commission didn't stand for anything they were being blamed for in the aftermath of the executive order. The commission wanted the reserves to be working forests, the public to be involved in discussions regarding their use, and the reserves to contribute to the prosperity of the western states. That those points were never conveyed was, in Pinchot's view, the fault of one man and his "inexcusable mishandling of the National Forest Commission."[13]

Pinchot was right. The commission's failure to provide recommendations for managing forest reserves along with their list of which lands deserved immediate protection put outgoing President Cleveland in a tough position and the prospects for wise forest conservation in peril. In short, the departing president's executive order establishing the new forest reserves had the effect of poking a beehive with a stick. Historian Robert Bassman described the ensuing chaos: "A storm of protest arose in the West, expressed in public meetings, memorials from legislatures, by letters from Western public officials, angry editorials and vituperative denunciation of the President in both Houses of Congress rarely equalled."[14]

The first days of the McKinley administration were consumed with the issue of whether the new reserves should be nullified—just six days after Cleveland's proclamation, an amendment had already been introduced in the Senate to do so. Because the National Forest Commission had not advanced ideas or worked with Congress to propose new laws regarding forest reserves, it meant that existing laws preventing any access or use were in effect for both the original and newly created areas.

Mining and timber interests were furious and demanded that the newly created reserves be returned to the public domain. The issue was so contentious that it was the "only question of public importance" discussed at the first full meeting of McKinley's cabinet.[15]

As the debate raged on, the National Forest Commission held meetings to hammer out their final report. Building consensus was difficult. In one full-day meeting, Pinchot noted in his diary that the group was able to gain a number of concessions from Sargent, but he refused to budge on the question of military control over the reserves. At other meetings, he wrote, "the civil war went on."[16] The going was so slow that by the time the report was issued on May 1, 1897, many of its recommendations had already been addressed by Congress.

The bill signed into law, known as the Organic Act of 1897, clarified that forest reservations could not be established for reasons other than protecting the forests or water sources within them or for supplying a continuous supply of timber. Further, it put the secretary of the interior in charge of making "such rules and regulations and establish[ing] such service as will ensure the objects of such reservations, namely, to regulate their occupancy and use and to preserve the forests therein from destruction."[17]

Pinchot, frustrated by the commission's entirely avoidable delays and failures, observed that if the National Forest Commission's report had been submitted on November 1, 1896, as originally requested by President Cleveland, "the attack in the Senate would have been impossible, the Reserves would not have had to be saved by the skin of their teeth, and in all likelihood they would not have been subjected to the political mismanagement of the Land Office for seven critical years."[18]

In public, Pinchot continued to be gracious in acknowledging Charles S. Sargent's contributions to forestry, but behind the scenes the two men sniped and quarreled. Sargent chided Pinchot for speaking on behalf of legislative compromises. Shortly after the Organic Act was signed into law in June 1897, Secretary of the Interior Cornelius N. Bliss offered Pinchot a job (which came to be called "confidential forest agent") for $1,200 per year. Pinchot renegotiated the terms to be $10 per day plus expenses and accepted. In his new role, Pinchot would study existing reserves, recommend necessary changes to their boundaries, and, most important, submit a proposal for the organization of a forest service.[19] Sargent was miffed at this development and chastised Pinchot for abandoning the cause of forestry in favor of siding with the politicians—the insinuation being that in doing so, he could ensure that his ideas would prevail over those officially presented by the National Forest Commission.

Dr. Dietrich Brandis, Pinchot's esteemed forestry school mentor, had also received a letter from Sargent leveling the same accusations. Grieved by what he had heard, Brandis wrote to Pinchot to encourage him to write a note of reconciliation, citing Sargent's two decades of work toward making the American practice of forestry a reality. Pinchot acquiesced, telling Sargent that he was "hopeful that the present misunderstanding may not continue."[20]

But continue it did. And the two would never speak to each other again.

CHAPTER TWELVE

Forester for Life

ON JULY 1, 1898, GIFFORD PINCHOT BECAME CHIEF OF THE FORESTRY Division. Five days later, he was delighted to learn that his boss, Secretary James Wilson, had given him the official title of "forester" as opposed to chief of division. In later life, Pinchot would recall his "great satisfaction" in obtaining this title. "I was a forester in fact before that happy day. I have since been a Governor, every now and then, but I am a forester all the time—have been, and shall be, all my working life," he said.[1]

When he took the helm of the Forestry Division, Pinchot faced two profound challenges. The first was that in the eighteen years since the agency was created, it had failed to control and manage any forest land at all. This created an even greater challenge—whether the agency would survive. A clause in the agricultural appropriation bill of 1898 called for the Forestry Division to make a case for its continued existence, a condition Pinchot blamed on his predecessor. Dr. Bernhard Fernow's view that the agency's role should be "a bureau of information" and his failure to provide "practical directions for applying forest management to American timberlands before they were cut" were major failings from Pinchot's perspective, going so far as to claim that Fernow was "one of the principal reasons why, before Biltmore Forest, there was no forest management in America."[2]

Wresting control of the existing preserves from the Department of the Interior's General Land Office would take time. But there were some things Pinchot could immediately take on to assert the department's influence, encourage implementation of sound forestry practices, and help slow the indiscriminate cutting of forests.

Because managing federal lands wasn't an option, Pinchot deftly turned his attention to where he could make the greatest immediate impact—with private and corporate timber holders. Just four months after he became the nation's head forester, the Division of Forestry published Circular No. 21, "to help farmers, lumbermen, and other private forest landowners to make working plans" for managing their forests.[3] Pinchot's plan was brilliant. As the first federal cooperative program to offer management assistance in the field, it offered forest management guidance at no cost to woodlot owners, whereas owners of larger tracts would pay the expenses of hosting government assistants in the field (exclusive of their salaries) and the cost of hiring local assistants.[4]

The program gave Pinchot's Department of Forestry the kick start it needed to become a relevant federal agency and then some. In its first year, lumber companies, farmers, and woodlot owners in thirty-five states were introducing forestry methods on a million and a half acres of wooded land.[5] Even more impressive was how much greater the demand for forestry stewardship advice exceeded the supply. With only "eight or ten American foresters" available to survey over four hundred thousand acres of forest in nineteen states, creating actionable plans was an impossible task. "We had turned on the water and we were like[ly] to be drowned," reported Pinchot.[6]

The Division of Forestry couldn't possibly keep up. Pinchot needed to hire some fresh recruits. Old Yale classmate, friend, and trained forester Henry Graves was one of the first to sign on. Then came Ralph Hosmer, Overton Price, and a long list of others who were "ultimately imbued with the fierce determination and zeal of their 'Chief' to halt the devastation of American forests."[7] Most worked for a salary of $25 per month plus traveling expenses, going up to $40 per month in the winter months, which they typically spent in Washington.[8] Additionally, many received financial help to get their careers started from Pinchot himself through promissory notes drawn for them on Riggs National Bank in Washington.[9]

By 1902, the young recruits, some thirty in number by now, fanned out to join lumber camps in the field, surveying land, recommending which trees should be cut or retained, and submitting reports back to the Division of Forestry.[10] The forestry management assistance program would only last another three years because events would soon transform the agency's responsibilities, but it had been successful in three ways. The ever action-oriented Pinchot had thrust a previously little-known agency into the public spotlight, he had empowered young foresters to carry the message of sustainable forestry practices to private landowners, and he had "brought forestry out of the office and lecture hall and into the woods where it helped to convince more Americans that forest use and protection were not incompatible."[11]

But Gifford Pinchot would not rest until the management of federal forest lands was under his control (an outcome he continually nurtured toward fruition through political outreach and public outcry). In the meantime, he foresaw the need to have more professionally trained foresters ready to join his growing ranks. Most important, he wanted them to understand, practice, and advocate for *his* methods of forestry.

CHAPTER THIRTEEN

A Profession Takes Root

THE FIRST FORESTRY SCHOOL IN AMERICA WAS ESTABLISHED ON THE grounds of the Biltmore Estate in 1898. The idea wasn't new. A dozen years earlier (and four years before he would be appointed secretary of the interior), Carl Schurz had proposed several actions to slow the rate of indiscriminate timber harvesting, including protecting timber by establishing preserves, creating laws for managing them, and establishing forestry schools.[1] Yet, as the twentieth century approached, there were still no such schools in America.

The main reason for the lack of schools was that the profession wasn't ready to hire a sufficient number of graduates. Publicly owned forests were only on the verge of regulation—the laws and means for enforcing them had yet to be established—so federal jobs were practically nil. The few nongovernment jobs available were offered by corporations and wealthy landowners who were becoming increasingly aware of the benefits of managing their forests. In this environment, it was no surprise that there were no forestry schools in existence, let alone ones looking for students. But there *were* students looking for them.

In 1894 when Gifford Pinchot's consulting business was growing, he came to realize that he would need help managing the Biltmore Forest. He suggested to George Vanderbilt that hiring a second forester to assist him would provide the day-to-day oversight the operation required to achieve profitability faster. The goal wasn't financial. Vanderbilt hardly needed money. They wanted to prove that managed forests were economically viable to help build national recognition and support for their creation. George Vanderbilt agreed, and Carl Schenck, who had earned a PhD from the renowned University of Giessen forestry school, was hired. Like Pinchot, Schenck had studied under Sir Dietrich Brandis, a pioneer of scientific forestry employed by the British Imperial Forest Service whose teachings and correspondence also influenced Franklin Hough, Charles Sargent, and Pinchot's friend Henry Graves.

When Pinchot took Schenck on a tour of the Biltmore Forest in 1895, the new arrival was awed by what he saw.

> *In the valley were the most beautiful trees I had ever seen. Towering tulip trees with gigantic chestnuts, red oaks, basswoods and ash trees at their feet. I soon realized that German forestry, the variety in which I had grown up, was as impossible in the United States as Indian or Swedish forestry. A brand new sort of forestry was needed.*[2]

Schenck's initial reaction was spot on. The mountains and valleys of North Carolina contained one of the most diverse forest habitats on earth. Over one hundred varieties of native trees thrived on its mountain slopes and moist temperate valleys. Managing the forest would be an incredible undertaking. Thanks to the work of Olmsted, Vanderbilt, and Pinchot, his objectives were clear. First was to repair the land. The overused agricultural lands surrounding the estate were to be transformed by planting them with trees to restore vegetation and prevent erosion. Second was the far more difficult task of proving that the practice of scientific forestry could produce a profit.

The first effort to harvest trees, a plan devised by Pinchot, was a financial and ecological debacle. The plan was to use "splash dams" (already a favored logging practice because it was one of the least expensive ways of getting wood out of the forest and to the mills). Building a series of temporary "splash dams" caused streams and rivers to flood. The reservoir created behind the highest dam would become the collection point for felled logs. A series of coordinated dam releases would then rush the logs downstream, where they could be collected near the mill.

Pinchot's plan (enthusiastically supported by Vanderbilt) was to harvest the mature stands of tulip poplar below Mount Pisgah. The massive trees would yield handsome profits, and eliminating the dense canopy they created would allow young saplings to grow quickly. To harvest the logs, Pinchot proposed flooding Big Creek by constructing splash dams, filling the resulting man-made reservoir with logs, then releasing them to rush downstream into the Mills River and finally the French Broad River, where the Biltmore's sawmill awaited their arrival.

With Pinchot off pursuing his new career as a forestry consultant, Schenck was left to implement the plan as his first job on the estate. Getting the logs into the reservoir was the only part of the project that worked. From then on, it was a cumulative disaster. The seventeen-foot logs became tangled and stuck in or near the former reservoir. Then heavy rains came, causing an enormous flood downstream, inundating local farmland and leaving logs stranded in the middle of fields after the water receded. The huge logs rushing downstream destroyed buildings and bridges. Although a few logs reached the French Broad River sawmill, the small profit they generated was no match for the physical and financial damage caused by the event.

Schenck was devastated. The lawsuits filed against the Biltmore Estate were an embarrassment and not an ideal way to impress his new boss. But even worse was his feeling that he had failed the forest by following a plan that preceded him. He wrote,

> Unique, unrivaled wonder trees had gone, and had gone forever. The primeval beauty of Big Creek had been destroyed. The financial loss incurred by our brand of forestry amounted to many thousands of dollars.[3]

The Big Creek project made Schenck rethink the way the Biltmore Forest should be managed. Selectively harvested trees would be henceforth moved to mills using roads, which would be cheaper in the long run, cause no further damage to watersheds, and make it easier to move foresters, equipment, and logs through the forest. It was a practice he called "permanent forestry."

Within two years, Schenck had the Biltmore Forest providing wood for customers in Asheville and beyond. He had also launched an enormous reforestation effort to reclaim the abused agricultural land surrounding the estate using native seedlings grown at the Biltmore nursery. He was meeting the objectives he was hired to implement, and he was putting scientific forestry to work in America.

As word of the forestry projects at Biltmore spread (aided no doubt by Pinchot's promotion of the cause), young men intent on becoming foresters began arriving at the estate. At first Schenck hired them as apprentices, taking them into the forest as he tended to his duties. As the number of new arrivals grew, it dawned on Schenck that he should start a forestry school.

In September 1898, Carl Schenck opened the Biltmore Forest School—the first of its kind in America. Schenck was convinced that teaching forestry was the greatest contribution he could make as a forester and to the future of the country's forests. To increase enrollment, he advertised the school in magazines under the headline "Knowledge Is the Best Money Maker."

The one-year courses were designed to equip students with an understanding of all parts of American forestry. There were no vacations. In the winter months, classes were held on the grounds of the estate. From spring through fall, they were held twenty miles away, deep in the forest, where Schenck repurposed an old school as a lecture hall and a scattering of surrounding cabins served as student housing. Visiting professors were brought in to teach dendrology, botany, geology, and other forestry-related subjects. Forest finance, entomology, and tree diseases were also part of the curriculum. Days were split between morning lectures and afternoon fieldwork. Schenck was a gifted teacher and leader who challenged his students to see forestry as an honorable profession that offered both a rewarding career and made a positive contribution to future generations. His students repaid him with their admiration and loyalty. One wrote, "The days . . . were replete with lessons derived from the lifework of Dr. Schenck—lessons in silviculture, ecology, utilization, protection and finance and that greater lesson of the value of energy, faith and firmness of conviction."[4]

In its first decade, the Schenck school thrived. Hundreds of students would become alumni, creating the first wave of state and federal foresters, researchers, and teachers. To celebrate that success, Schenck arranged a special event he named the Biltmore Forest Fair. He sent a personal letter and a fifty-five-page, self-designed illustrated brochure to nearly four hundred invitees. Prominent politicians (including every member of Congress), lumbermen, engineers, and other influential guests were invited to come to the Biltmore Estate to "learn from the forest, rather than from the books."[5]

The pamphlet's introduction read simply,

> What "Biltmore Forest" is—
> I cannot describe;
> Nor can this booklet tell you.
> See for yourself, my friend,
> And use the "tips" as guides,
> Which I present to you
> Herewith.
> Respectfully,
> THE FORESTER

The pamphlet highlighted forestry practices within different parts of the forest and nursery. It also included financial statements detailing expenses, income, and net profit.

The three-day event drew attendees from as far away as Wisconsin, Texas, and the province of Quebec and included "botanists, forest engineers, lumbermen, furniture manufacturers, state foresters, statesmen, editors, paper company representatives, university professors and others."[6]

The *Southern Lumberman* declared that the fair "marked an epoch in American forestry" and noted that "so unique and original were Dr. Schenck's methods of carrying out the program that during the entire Festival there was never one who lagged behind or lost interest, or was not looking forward with eager anticipation to the next event."[7]

The Biltmore Forest Fair was an important building block in the creation of a national forestry movement, introducing most of those on hand and yet thousands more through his mailings and the press to the possibilities of professionally managed forests. "For the first time in their lives, they had seen real forestry in America," said Schenck, who referred to the event as the highlight of his career.[8]

But Schenck's time at the Biltmore Estate would last only one more year. After a series of disagreements with George Vanderbilt about how the forest should be managed (and, as we shall see, influenced by Pinchot's input), he resigned as the estate's chief forester. Schenck kept the school operating for another few years, using American and European forests as his classrooms, but he ceased operations in the fall of 1913. In his final *Biltmore Doings* newsletter of January 1914, Schenck poignantly lamented, "To-day lumbering is supposed to be taught, in one way or other, at no less than 83 American schools. There seems to be no more need, therefore, of a unique school like the Biltmore Forest School. . . . [The enrollments] have been so small, recently, that its continuance is not worth while. . . . I am sorry for my boys; I had meant to lead them to victory; I have led them to sorrow, and their Alma Mater is about to die."[9]

Two of the aforementioned eighty-three schools would play a particularly important and immediate role in the trajectory of American forestry.

THE RUSH TO CREATE FORESTRY SCHOOLS

The New York State College of Forestry at Cornell (which began the same year as the Biltmore Forest School) was created by an act of the New York legislature and became the first four-year forestry school in the country in 1898.

The Adirondack Forest Preserve's "forever wild" provision never sat well with the state's first superintendent of forests. Colonel William Fox, who was from a lumbering family, had studied forestry in Germany and had been "unceasing in his attempts to purchase as much land for the [Adirondack] preserve as possible."[10] But his efforts weren't aimed at preservation. He believed "that the State's constitutional amendment setting aside the Adirondack and Catskill preserves as lands to be kept forever wild was unfortunate."[11] Like Gifford Pinchot, whose appeals to manage the preserves as working forests failed, Colonel Fox felt that the electorate who voted in favor of "forever wild" protection simply didn't understand the positive implications of professional forest management. In the years since the preserve had been established, other voices chimed in, including Charles Sargent and Bernhard Fernow, who told the New York Chamber of Commerce in 1888 that state ownership and "fully equipped, rational forest management" were the only means to save and restore "favorable forest conditions" in the Adirondacks.[12]

While like-minded individuals and organizations favored the practice of professional forestry within the preserve, Fox recognized there was no public appetite for it. Thus, he began working toward a means of proving to the public what modern forestry could achieve. Eventually his plan for a demonstration forest caught the ear of a Cornell University trustee, who suggested that a forest managed by the school might pass legislative muster. Cornell president Jacob Gould Schurman embraced the idea and turned to Pinchot, Schenck, and Fernow for technical advice.

The state legislature approved the creation of the New York State College of Forestry in 1898, with the stipulation that Cornell University would hold the title, possession, management, and control of the acquired land for thirty years, at which time it would revert to state ownership. The implications of this arrangement started playing out quickly and would profoundly affect the course of forestry in America.

First, Gifford Pinchot's adversary, Dr. Bernhard Fernow, was recruited to be the dean of the college. Upon accepting the job, he resigned his position as chief of the Forestry Division within the Department of Agriculture. Pinchot was swiftly offered Fernow's old job, but he hesitated to take it, even asking the secretary of agriculture James Wilson if he could work in the Adirondacks for three more years while the Forestry Division job was held for him. After further consultation with his father, Professor William H. Brewer (his National Forest Commission cohort), and Henry Graves, who agreed to become Pinchot's assistant in the division, he "came to [his] senses and realized that here was the chance of a lifetime."[13]

Meanwhile, in Upstate New York, the School of Forestry of Cornell University immediately headed down the path toward controversy. Fernow's first task was to find a suitable parcel of forest to manage. He settled on acquiring a thirty-thousand-acre tract that was owned by one of the major lumber companies in the region, the Santa Clara Lumber Company. The purchase was paid for with $165,000 provided by the state, per the legislation that created the school. A bonus for Fernow and Cornell was that part of the parcel had served as a lumber camp, complete with buildings that could be immediately used to house students and equipment.

As the school was appropriated only $10,000 per year, Fernow sought additional means of financial support. Ralph S. Hosmer, one of the early foresters (hired by Gifford Pinchot in 1898), recalled hearing that Fernow had met with (then New York governor) Theodore Roosevelt in Albany. As the story went, when Roosevelt asked Fernow, "How are you getting on?" Fernow replied, "Well, pretty well I think if the legislature would give me some money to work with." Hearing this, Roosevelt reportedly wrote a note on a card saying, "Give this man what he wants"; he handed the card to Fernow and told him, in turn, to hand the card to a certain member of a powerful state committee. However, Fernow never followed up on the offer, later saying, "Of course, I never did that because I would be introducing politics into the game and that's what I was trying to keep away from."[14] Fernow would quickly discover how naive a decision that was, especially with the politically astute, well-connected Gifford Pinchot already playing the game at the highest level.

The forester was determined to show that a managed forest could be profitable. With a New York State appropriation of only $10,000 per year, generating sustainable income from timber harvests became his highest priority. At Fernow's behest, the university signed a contract with the Brooklyn Cooperage Company in the nearby village of Tupper Lake, who would buy hardwood from the school's forest for their manufacture of barrel staves. Fernow had a six-mile rail line built for transporting logs to the company's plant. The harvested hardwoods would be replaced by pine and Norway spruce seedlings from the school's nursery. Ideally, the relationship would benefit both parties. As it turned out, the cooperage was the clear winner. The first attempts to establish seedlings yielded dismal results—a particularly harsh winter resulted in severe losses. In the end, the school wouldn't even raise enough money to fully replant their clear-cuts.

Fernow's prior decisions may have been ill advised, but his determination to have the brush piles left in the wake of harvest set on fire ignited a public relations disaster. "The smoke drifted toward Upper Saranac Lake where wealthy camp owners rushed to Wawbeek [the site of the harvest] to see what was going on. They neither understood nor liked what they saw, and with influential contacts in Albany halted the project and had Fernow fired."[15]

The School of Forestry of Cornell University lasted only five years. In 1903, Governor Benjamin B. Odell made a pocket veto of the school's annual appropriation, noting that the school had "practically denuded the forest lands of the State without compensating benefits."[16] Soon after, the school decided to cease operations.

Ironically, the project designed to demonstrate the benefits of scientific forestry left a damaging impression. After the Brooklyn Cooperage Company lost an appeal to the New York Supreme Court attempting to hold Cornell to its contract, esteemed lawyer and Adirondack landowner and preservationist Louis Marshall (father of Bob Marshall, whom we shall meet in a later chapter) said that "the consequence of that [arrangement] was that this 'tremendous' tract of thirty thousand acres was to be cut down 'flat' from one end of it to the other, in order that the scientific foresters might start a new forest which might mature a hundred years from [when the] contract was entered into. This is scientific forestry?"[17]

In the aftermath of the debacle, the thirty-thousand-acre demonstration forest was absorbed back into the preserve and designated as "forever wild," a status preserved to this day.

One School Thrives

In 1900, another forestry school was established under the auspices of a university. This one would go on to provide a steady supply of American foresters for generations to come. Given its origins, it is easy to see why its success was assured.

In February of that year, the Pinchot family endowed Yale University with $150,000 to establish a two-year master's program in forestry. The idea for the school had come into being the decade before when Gifford was studying in Europe, the only place then offering forestry instruction. But the creation of the school was not merely a magnanimous gesture to Gifford's alma mater. It was also part of their plan for "outspending, outwitting and outmaneuvering" competitive forestry schools "while working to establish their vision of scientific forestry in America."[18]

Pinchot's efforts to discredit the Biltmore Forestry School and to have Carl Schenck fired from Vanderbilt's employ began in earnest after the Yale Forest School was up and running. It was only two years after Schenck had established the Biltmore Forest School "with Vanderbilt's consent and Pinchot's encouragement" that Schenck was turned aside.[19] Pinchot's campaign began with private talks with Vanderbilt but also went public on the printed page.

Shortly after the U.S. Bureau of Forestry was established in 1901 (and Pinchot became its head), Schenck wrote an article for the *American Lumberman* magazine. In it, he questioned the ability of the federal government to adequately manage its forest holdings in the American South without having a precise inventory of the timber it owned. In a subsequent issue of the same magazine, an article written by the chief geographer of the U.S. Geological Survey, Henry Gannett, held Schenck's suggestion of a field inventory of southern forest lands up for ridicule. When Schenck asked Gannett, whom he knew as both a colleague and a "devoted friend of forestry," why he would write such "discrediting" remarks about him, Gannett replied that it was at the request of Gifford Pinchot.[20] Schenck was understandably stunned. Years later he would recall his disappointment. He "had thought Pinchot incapable of such action," particularly because he had helped Pinchot on several projects over the years. "True, I had criticized some of Pinchot's activities in my lectures on forest policy, and I had advised my graduates to seek employment with the large owners of timberlands rather than the Bureau of Forestry in Washington, because I wanted them to be foresters in the woods rather than foresters in office buildings," recalled Schenck. "But I had never published, nor said in public, anything disparaging to him."[21]

The last sentence, written with such conviction, was hard to square with the fact that Schenck had questioned the methods of an agency under Pinchot's direction in a trade journal and in lectures regarding forest policy. Nonetheless, this was the same Gifford Pinchot who had hired Schenck on the advice of one of his forestry heroes, Sir Dietrich Brandis; had welcomed Schenck to America by taking him on a grand tour of New York

City; and had subsequently proclaimed, "Dr. Schenck, I believe you are just the right man for the position" (of forester of the Biltmore Estate).[22]

Although Schenck felt blindsided, the events that led to his ousting from the Biltmore Estate had in truth been envisioned and then engineered by Gifford Pinchot and family over several years. As early as 1890, when Gifford was studying forestry in Europe, he and his father were discussing the need for such a school in America. Four years later, James upped the ante, relating that he felt that the family should help create the first forestry school in America and that he had "spoken with a Pennsylvania senator about a plan."[23]

Bernard Fernow had identified the need for a college forestry program as early as 1887, but there wasn't enough demand for foresters to make such a program feasible. Just eleven years later, the landscape had changed. With the profitability (and regulation) of forestry assured and the need for professional foresters nigh, Fernow resigned as chief of the U.S. Department of Agriculture's Division of Forestry to lead the New York State College of Forestry.

The establishment of two schools teaching forestry was enough to speed the creation of the Yale program. And the projected need for foresters wasn't the only impetus. Pinchot and his right-hand man at the Division of Forestry (fellow Yale graduate Henry Graves) had hired college attendees and graduates to help with administrative duties and fieldwork but agreed that advance training in forestry would be a real plus to the bureau. Further, they aspired to create a "Yale program to supersede Fernow's school at Cornell."[24] Pinchot's rocky relationship with Fernow may have played a role in their quest to diminish his stature, but publicly, Pinchot declared that it was the style of forestry practiced by both Fernow and Schenck that drove the Pinchots to establish the Yale program as the best in America.

Pinchot and Graves felt that the German methods of forestry practiced by Fernow and Schenck were suspect, with Pinchot even going as far as saying that both lacked faith in American forestry.[25] Another irreconcilable difference was that Schenck believed students should work for private landowners to gain experience before working for the government. Schenck particularly bemoaned that Roosevelt and Pinchot had antagonized and attacked "lumber barons" as "enemies of the United States."[26] The argument boiled over on one of Pinchot's visits to the Biltmore Nurseries, where the two quarreled for an hour on the topic, culminating in Pinchot calling Schenck "the antichrist."[27]

By 1909, Schenck had been dispatched from the Biltmore Estate. Undeterred, he attempted to keep the Biltmore School afloat by holding classes throughout the United States and Europe. But, as he discovered, an unprofitable school lacking a degree program could not compete with the growing number of accredited schools, especially one backed by a $150,000 endowment (which would soon grow to $300,000) and that offered a direct path to employment with a federal agency.

The Yale Forest School greeted its first students in the summer of 1901. Classes were held at Grey Towers (the Pinchot estate) and Forest Hall, an impressive stone lecture hall with classrooms funded by James Pinchot in Milford, Pennsylvania, just down the hill. The school would continue to operate on the estate for more than twenty-five years. The

The Yale Forest School conducted classes at the Pinchot estate. Students were housed in tents pitched in the forest behind the family home. (Author photo)

sixty acres of woods at Grey Towers was where hundreds of future foresters would acquire the skills needed to bring a new profession into being
just as their services were urgently required.

On this point, Henry Graves, who became the first dean of the
school, said that "the object of the school was not only to give specific
instruction but to build up a profession; not merely to teach men how
to handle forest lands, but to train them to be leaders in one of the most
important economic movements of the time."[28]

As educators, Graves and Pinchot (who also served as a professor
of forestry at the school) were directly shaping the future of American
forestry and planting the seeds for succession. From 1905 to 1940, every
head of the Forest Service was a graduate of the Yale Forest School.
Also important to Pinchot was that the school was "instrumental in
establishing standards for American forestry education and supplying
many teachers for new forest schools that soon sprang up all over the
country."[29]

In the end, Gifford Pinchot's determination, political savvy, influential
connections, and considerable wealth combined to ensure that his vision
for forestry in the United States would be the one that prevailed. In the
first years of the 1900s, as the Yale Forest School began producing its first
graduates, Gifford Pinchot was ready and able to put them to work.

AS FOR FERNOW AND SCHENCK . . .

After the demise of their respective schools, Bernhard Fernow and Carl
Schenck would both leave America. Upon the closing of the New York
State College of Forestry at Cornell, Fernow taught forestry for one
semester at Pennsylvania State University, then left the country to head
the forestry department at the University of Toronto.

Carl Schenck moved to his homeland of Germany. In 1950, at the
behest of former students, he returned to North Carolina for an alumni
reunion, where he was honored with forests named after him and a com-
memorative plaque that would become known as the "Plymouth Rock
of Forestry," placed at the site of his forest classrooms. Shortly before his
death, he wrote, "I myself have so much cause to be grateful that I feel I
should be walking on my knees, rather than on my feet."[30]

Chapter Fourteen

MacKaye Charts His Course

By 1897, at age eighteen (just four years after his father's quite unexpected death), Benton MacKaye headed off to college. During the next four years, several themes emerged that would shape the rest of Benton MacKaye's life. The first was following a narrow path of interests. Benton was never destined to be a well-rounded student. At Harvard, his best subjects were English and geology, where he earned Bs and Cs.[1] It is hardly surprising because MacKaye's preferred form of education was through experiential learning. He favored hosting or attending informal gatherings to discuss social and political philosophy or exploring the hills of New England to sitting in lecture halls. Structured working environments would present challenges to him for the rest of his life. He was much better suited to and happiest when he was charting his own course. "Following his own interests in his own manner," geography, forestry, and regional planning had become his callings, and he would always find employment in those professions.[2] But earning a salary from them that would support both him and eventually his sister Hazel would be the most enduring challenge of all. Indeed, it would shape his personal and professional decisions until his death at age ninety-four. (The precarious financial condition the death of his father brought on the family likely contributed to this lifelong focus and concern.)

A far more exciting draw, which would be the greatest influence on his life, was donning his boots to explore the forests and mountains of his native New England, where both his classroom studies and his spirit came to life. After his freshman year in August 1897, he set out on his inaugural adventure into the high peaks of New Hampshire's White Mountains. He could not have known at the time that the very mountains he traversed would be central to his achievements and enduring legacy. His companions on the trip were Harvard classmates Draper Maury and Sturgis Pray (who would ultimately work for the Olmsted Brothers firm as a landscape architect).

Just getting to the start of the team's hike was a journey unto itself—a ten-day bike ride from the MacKaye home in Shirley, Massachusetts, into the heart of the White Mountains in 1897 was unquestionably ambitious—but nothing compared to the hike Benton would remember as the moment he "first saw the true wilderness."[3]

MacKaye's hiking partners where both twenty-six and were familiar with the region. Sturgis Pray had joined the Appalachian Mountain Club (whose affiliation with the White Mountains began with its founding in 1876) when he was eighteen. Initiating their hike from the Swift River Valley was almost certainly on Pray's recommendation and informed his oversight of the construction of the Swift River Trail, which MacKaye would help him build five years later.

MacKaye noted that his first trip through the Swift River Valley was as beautiful a sight as he had seen, but a greater experience awaited on top of Mount Tremont. After spending a day bushwhacking to the summit ridge and enduring a thorough soaking by a summer rainstorm, Benton and his mates scrambled to the summit ridge to witness the peaks rising through the clouds and vistas as far flung as Maine to the east and Massachusetts to the south. As one historian noted, "It was at that moment, as the sun rose and the weather cleared, that MacKaye would always remember as one of revelation, perhaps the closest thing to a religious experience that he ever mentioned or recorded."[4]

The 1897 trip would be the first of eight annual pilgrimages Benton MacKaye would make to the New England mountains and countryside. They likely would have continued had it not been for his profession taking him further afield. Two of those adventures stand out thanks to the benefits of historical context.

In mid-July of 1900, MacKaye and his Harvard classmate Horace Hildreth took a train to southern Vermont, then spent the bulk of the next two weeks exploring the Green Mountains. Their objective was to climb to as many of the state's high summits as possible. (Initially, they were joined by Benton's brother, Percy, who departed one week into the trip after the trio had climbed Haystack, Stratton, and Bromley Mountains.) Relying on the generosity of locals, who often fed the young explorers and provided spartan accommodations, the duo went on to climb Camel's Hump and the state's highest peak, Mount Mansfield (4,393 feet). Almost fifty-five years later, MacKaye would recall that the view gained from one of the mountaintops on this trip, during his twenty-first year, was so expansive that it inspired him to think about the possibility of creating a footpath that would make hiking to those distant summits possible.[5]

Between 1897 and 1903, Benton MacKaye frequently rendezvoused with his mentor, Sturgis Pray, who was overseeing trail construction in the White Mountains as an officer of the Appalachian Mountain Club. In the summer of 1903, MacKaye joined Pray's crew to build the Swift River Trail, an important "trunk line connecting the Bartlett, Chocorua, Tamworth, and Wonalancet paths with routes to Waterville and Livermore," with plans for extending the trail well beyond.[6] The Swift River Trail was historic, for it was the first effort in the region to connect disparate trail systems with a central path. Before Pray's idea came to fruition, trails had typically been constructed as "out and back" footpaths. Bringing a landscape architect's perspective

Sturgis Pray, circa 1915–1920.
(Bain Collection, Library of Congress)

to trail design and maintenance was revolutionary. (Pray studied under Olmsted Jr. and would succeed him as chairman of the Department of Landscape Architecture at Harvard University, a post he would hold until the year before his death in 1929 at fifty-seven years old.)

The Swift River Trail "was a landmark in the history of the White Mountains recreational landscape,"[7] and Benton MacKaye was one of the trail builders who made the trail come to life. There is no doubt that MacKaye benefited from his mentor's influence. In MacKaye's words, Sturgis Pray was a "Moses in reverse [that] led me *into* the wilderness."[8]

"Sturgis Pray's personal and practical influence on MacKaye's ideas about hiking trails cannot be overstated," said MacKaye biographer Larry Anderson. "Not only did Pray introduce MacKaye to the techniques, rigors, and outright fun of mountain tramping. He also enunciated the standards and principles of trail design that Benton unequivocally adopted."[9]

Importantly, Pray's genius extended beyond *where* trails should be constructed to *how* they should be constructed. He believed in treading lightly on the land. In a 1952 interview, MacKaye recalled that Sturgis Pray had showed him "how to have a path, a line of accessibility, and also have a 'wood'—a wilderness minus the marks of man."[10] As a "pioneer in keeping improvements *out* of the wilderness," Pray had shaped MacKaye's "first notions of what constitutes a true wilderness path."[11] It was a lesson MacKaye would embrace and share with others for the rest of his life.

But in 1902, there was a more pressing issue for Benton MacKaye than hiking and trail building. He needed to find a vocation that would produce steady income. Making his way as a tutor in New York City in the winter months and a summer camp counselor in the summers had run their respective courses. He briefly dreamed about starting a seafaring summer camp, but a near-death experience with appendicitis (complete with an emergency operation on the kitchen table illuminated by kerosene lanterns) convinced him that Sturgis Pray's suggestion to become a forester held both financial and philosophical appeal.

While MacKaye would credit both Pray and Maury for helping him steer toward a career in forestry, their advice was less revelatory and more acts of urging their friend to continue along the career path he was already blazing. Benton confided to his brother James that "for several years now I have been trying to work out some method whereby I could make a living in those lines that interested me."[12]

When Gifford Pinchot delivered a lecture at Harvard on March 2, 1900, and MacKaye heard the nation's leading forester make the case for "the great need for intelligent supervision of the country's forests, and for trained men to carry on this work,"[13] he wasn't yet ready to respond. But his hiking and cycling trips in Vermont and New Hampshire (the first one occurring just four months after Pinchot's lecture) had exposed MacKaye to large logging operations that were felling trees on a massive scale. Like Sturgis Pray, MacKaye came to fear that logging operations would "render the future beauty of our paths uncertain" and that "more far-seeing forestry methods . . . by the inauguration of national control"[14] needed to be established.

The more he thought about it, the more MacKaye realized that a career in forestry would combine his interests in being outdoors, studying the landscape, developing forestry management plans, and writing. Maury and Pray were simply the encouraging voices that prompted him to take action.

Yale was the obvious choice, and MacKaye started looking into attending his second Ivy League school. His return letter from Director Henry Graves, the man hand-chosen by Pinchot to run the school, was only partially encouraging. Instead of attending the Yale Forestry School, he suggested that MacKaye look into a different program (one he hadn't been aware of until he received Grave's letter)—the new forestry program taking shape at his alma matter, Harvard University. MacKaye quickly enrolled, and in 1905 he would be the first to receive a degree in forestry from the school. His timing couldn't have been better. For in Washington, DC, the Division of Forestry was hiring, and Benton MacKaye became a forest assistant in Gifford Pinchot's department. His first steady job, developing plans for managing forests, promised a $1,000 annual salary. Benton MacKaye's mental and physical wanderings had finally paid off.

CHAPTER FIFTEEN

Gifford Pinchot's Department

TWO YEARS INTO HIS TENURE AS THE NATION'S HEAD FORESTER, GIF-
ford Pinchot continued to be a valued forestry management adviser with
no forests under his active management. But due to his well-known perseverance and political savvy, that was about to change.

Unlike his rival Bernhard Fernow, who had decided against getting
help from then governor Theodore Roosevelt in 1898 because it would be
"introducing politics into the game," Pinchot felt the opposite. In 1897,
Roosevelt nominated the aspiring forester to become a member of the
Boone and Crockett hunting club (which Roosevelt himself had founded
ten years before). The two became fast friends, and Pinchot's forestry principles gained an eager audience with the conservation-minded governor—so
much so that Pinchot convinced him to streamline the New York State
Forest Commission.[1] It was the beginning of a partnership that would literally redefine conservation in America. But there would be steps in between.

In 1900, shortly after Roosevelt became vice president, and undoubtedly influenced by Pinchot, he called for a vast expansion of national
forest reserves, insisting that the prosperity of the West, and indeed the
entire country, were dependent on the preservation of forests.[2]

In Roosevelt's first annual message to Congress as president in
December 1901 (McKinley had been assassinated in September, thus
Roosevelt sent the address rather than appearing before the houses), he
renewed his call for more forest reserves, emphasizing that their creation,
backed by sound management practices, would "enable the reserves to
contribute their full share to the people and give more assurance of future

resources."[3] It is hard to imagine that Roosevelt's assurances to ranchers, miners, and lumber interests were not informed by Pinchot, who was still miffed about the entirely avoidable response to President Cleveland's Forest Reserve proclamation a few years before—a debacle he laid entirely at the feet of Charles S. Sargent.

Most important to Gifford Pinchot was Roosevelt's case for consolidating the government's forestry departments and placing them under Pinchot's management (the draft language for which came from Pinchot himself).[4] Roosevelt wrote to Congress that,

> at present the protection of the forest reserves rests with the General Land Office, the mapping and description of their timber with the United States Geological Survey, and the preparation of plans for their conservative use with the Bureau of Forestry, which is also charged with the general advancement of practical forestry in the United States. These various functions should be united in the Bureau of Forestry, to which they properly belong.
>
> The present diffusion of responsibility is bad from every standpoint. It prevents that effective co-operation between the Government and the men who utilize the resources of the reserves, without which the interests of both must suffer. The scientific bureaus generally should be put under the Department of Agriculture. The President should have by law the power of transferring lands for use as forest reserves to the Department of Agriculture.[5]

It would take another four years for the move to be made, but Roosevelt had presented a rational case for doing so to both his congressional audience and the American people at large. (Interestingly, in the same speech, avid outdoorsman Roosevelt also urged that "certain of the forest reserves should also be made preserves for the wild forest creatures,"[6] likely the first time a president called for the creation of designated wilderness areas in a public speech.)

Reflecting on the importance of Roosevelt's first address to Congress, Pinchot said it was "a landmark in the development of forestry in the United States," for it gave forestry "a new standing that was invaluable," such that everyone, "in Congress and out, might know that the Administration was behind us."[7]

That was so, but even the backing of Roosevelt at his bully best could not speed the desired transfer of lands to the Department of Agriculture. The voices of protest ranged from ranchers, miners, and timber company owners who benefited from the status quo to senators who questioned the worth of scientific forestry, to agency heads loath to cede control of federal forests or forest policies to a competing department.

In March 1904, Pinchot called his top Bureau of Forestry assistants to a meeting. They determined that a national forestry conference might hold the key to the agency reorganization they coveted. Pinchot would later write that the American Forest Conference "was planned, organized and conducted for the specific purpose of the transfer by the Bureau of Forestry" of federal forest reserves to the Department of Agriculture. If (finally) enacted, the transfer would give Pinchot administrative control of over eighty-six million acres of forest reserves, ensuring that, in his words, "they might be handled under the principles of practical Forestry in the light of local facts and local needs, and so be given their fullest usefulness, now and hereafter."[8]

Held January 2–6, 1905, the American Forest Congress was able to deliver the far-reaching support Gifford Pinchot had been working toward for seven years. More than four hundred leaders representing timber, railroad, livestock, and mining interests attended, as well as congressmen, senators, and representatives of various government agencies. Conference secretary William L. Hall reported that "attendance was large, interest keen in every session. [The conference] fixed attention on forest conservation as a national program of high importance. . . . Gifford Pinchot's mastery of this great meeting was evident to all. It made him the national leader in forestry and related phases of conservation."[9]

The American Forest Congress concluded with a keynote speech by Theodore Roosevelt. Addressing attendees of the conference from the stage of the National Theatre, he said,

You have made, by your coming [to this congress], a meeting which is without parallel in the history of forestry. For the first time the

great business and the forest interests of the Nation have joined together . . . to consider their individual and their common interests in the forest. . . . Our country, we have faith to believe, is only at the beginning of its growth. Unless the forests of the United States can be made ready to meet the vast demands which this growth will inevitably bring, commercial disaster, that means disaster to the whole country, is inevitable.[10]

He concluded his remarks by specifically aiming at those attendees representing western states, who had been skeptical about federal forest management.

Unless [you] believe in forest preservation, the western forests cannot be preserved. . . . We believe, we know, that it is essential for the well-being of the people of the States of the Great Plains, the States of the Rockies, the States of the Pacific slope, that the forests shall be preserved, and we know also that our belief will count for nothing unless the people of those States themselves wish to preserve the forests. If they do, we can help them materially; we can direct their efforts, but we cannot save the forests unless they wish them to be saved.[11]

In his autobiography, Pinchot declared that "what was most important about the Forest Congress was the new recruits whom we had won over to our side"[12]—the presidents of the Great Northern Railroad and the Northern Pacific and the titans of the lumber industry (including F. E. Weyerhaeuser) among them. The backing of those new recruits helped propel the passage of H.R. 8460, the Transfer Act. Only twenty-six days after the American Forest Conference concluded, President Roosevelt received the bill from Congress and signed it into law.

"What I had been hoping for and working for, from the moment I came into the Forestry Division nearly seven long years before, had finally arrived," said Pinchot. "It had been a long pull, and, as it turned out, a strong pull. Now it had to be a pull all together, if we were to make good use of the chance which perseverance, common sense, T.R., and the American Forest Congress had given us."[13]

The Roosevelt/Pinchot partnership placed millions of
acres of forests under federal control. Photo 1907.
(U.S. Fish and Wildlife Service)

It was also time to lead a new workforce, comprised of his existing
staff and an additional 570 employees he'd inherited from the Land
Office, into a new era of forest management.

THE CHIEF TAKES CHARGE

On the day Pinchot took charge of what would soon be officially named
the "U.S. Forest Service," he was issued a letter signed by Secretary of
Agriculture "Tama Jim" Wilson containing the final version of the Transfer Act, as signed by the president, requesting swift input regarding the
rules and regulations required by the act and establishing the "purpose
and spirit of the new enterprise." The letter, composed by Pinchot him-

self, included the following passage, which would become the guiding principle of the Forest Service for Pinchot's tenure and beyond:

> *In the administration of the forest reserves it must be clearly borne in mind that all land is to be devoted to its most productive use for the permanent good of the whole people, and not for the temporary benefit of individuals or companies.*[14]

Thanks to Pinchot's foresight, there was no shortage of foresters trained in his way of thinking to help implement the Forest Service's business. But running an efficient operation with headquarters in Washington, DC, and field stations exclusively located in western states (eastern national forests would not be established for several years) brought significant challenges.

The way Pinchot saw it, his first order of business was hiring the right people, and the second was giving them the means to do the job. A critical tool for doing so was a field manual. Pinchot and his team went to work. Hosting writing and revision sessions at his house that often extended through the night and past breakfast, they created a book titled *The Use of National Forest Reserves: Regulations and Instructions*. Bound in cloth and sent to officers in the field in advance of the regulations therein (which went into effect on July 1, 1905), the "Use Book" standardized policy and conduct for the service, setting the standard for an effective operation. More than a book of regulations, the Use Book also provided guidance for professional behavior ("Forest Officers will be required to be thoroughly familiar with every part of this book, and to instruct the public and assist in making applications for the use of the reserves"[15]).

As Pinchot's band of foresters set off to manage America's forests—most prepared with a forestry degree and all with a set of clearly defined regulations and a code of conduct to uphold—they also toiled with an uncommon sense of purpose, thanks to the man they affectionately referred to as "Chief."

Ralph Hosmer, the seventh person hired by Pinchot to join the then Bureau of Forestry in 1898, recalled that "forestry was a cause in those days. All of us who followed Pinchot were so impressed by what he stood for and his magnetic way of drawing men to him. Anything that Pinchot said was right; there was no question about it, Pinchot had said it. We followed him through fire and flood."[16]

Clarence Dunston recalled arriving at Forest Service Atlantic Building headquarters in Washington in 1906 for training before being assigned to work in one of the national forests. "The spirit of youth pervaded the Atlantic Building at that time," he wrote. "Our Chief, Gifford Pinchot, was still a young man. Several men holding imposing titles as Division Chiefs were in their mid-twenties. I am sure that every one of us young Forest Assistants started out to his field post, after that brief inspirational training course, fired with the determination to do his utmost to forward the cause of conservation in the United States."[17]

But the changes brought about by the Transfer Act also placed some foresters in untenable, even dangerous positions. In a letter he wrote to Pinchot in 1939, forester Shirley "C. J." Buck recalled the reception he received by miners in 1906 when he worked in California's Klamath National Forest:

> *The resentment against the Government coming into the situation was so strong that an attempt was made to elect local congressmen on the basis of fighting the Forest Service. Life was a little strenuous for a new green forester since I was new to the National Forests and the miners spent part of their day times in reading the* Use Book *and consulting lawyers so they could ask me embarrassing questions on my return each night to town from [timber] cruising. I quickly found myself studying the* Use Book *in bed in an attempt to at least keep up with the information status of the local people on National Forest subjects. . . . They threatened to have something happen to me like pushing me off the bridge into the Klamath River, which idea they gave up solely through a realization that other men would come along to the work I was doing. They felt it would be an endless chain and was not worth the trouble and risk.*[18]

One reason that the chief's staff continued to stick with him through hard, even threatening times was the knowledge that he stood behind them. Pinchot entrusted them to carry out their mission, believing that "the Forest Service was no organization of master and servant. It was a service of mutual effort for a common purpose. We were all working together to the same end."[19]

That common purpose entailed more than assuming the management of the nation's enormous forest holdings and enforcing new policies that were, in some cases, unpopular. The support generated at the American Forest Congress from representatives of the paper and railroad industries had helped buy Pinchot some time with them, but others were suspicious, agitated, or downright hostile toward the newly comprised government agency.

Pinchot felt that the best way for the U.S. Forest Service to prove its worth was to demonstrate "that Forestry was good business and could actually be made to pay"[20]—the same principle that had been guiding him since the Biltmore Forest days. But proving it would take time. And the complaints in some quarters were gaining momentum. Mining interests pointed to an increased cost of doing business, citing permitting fees and regulatory requirements. Timber interests charged that timber sales from federal lands promoted competition with private lumbering. The voices of protest increased to the point of Pinchot being depicted as "Czar Pinchot" in speeches and political cartoons.[21]

The issue moved from the pages of newspapers and the lecterns of lecture halls into the halls of Congress in early 1907 when Oregon senator Charles W. Fulton introduced an amendment to the Agricultural Appropriation Bill of 1907 stating, "Hereafter no forest reserve shall be created, nor shall any addition be made to one heretofore created, within the limits of the States of Oregon, Washington, Idaho, Montana, Colorado or Wyoming except by an act of Congress."[22]

If passed, the amendment would strip the president's power to create forest reserves, established in 1891, and transfer that power to Congress. Neither the president nor Pinchot was pleased, but Roosevelt was in a quandary. He needed the appropriations bill to pass so the federal government could keep operating, and he had one week before the deadline to sign the bill into law.

Pinchot came up with a plan. Realizing this could well be their last chance to acquire federal land in six western states (and upon getting Roosevelt's "enthusiastic support"), Pinchot and his staff in Washington and in the field worked around the clock to identify tracts that they felt should become federal lands. Before signing the 1907 agriculture appropriation bill, Roosevelt signed a series of executive orders creating twenty-one new national forests and augmenting several existing ones— adding some sixteen million acres of land to the federal holdings, infuriating the creators of the amendment, and, in Pinchot's words, rescuing the lands from "passing into the hands of private corporations."[23]

Why Pinchot felt it was so important to gain control of the federal lands was a moral issue, one essential to preserving America's democracy. In his 1910 book, *The Fight for Conservation*, he wrote,

> *The central thing for which Conservation stands is to make this country the best possible place to live in, both for us and our descendants. It stands against the waste of the natural resources which cannot be renewed, such as coal and iron; it stands for the perpetuation of the resources that can be renewed, such as the food-producing soils and the forests; and most of all it stands for an equal opportunity for every American citizen to get his fair share of benefit from these resources, both now and hereafter.*[24]

The transfer of lands engineered by Pinchot and made official by Roosevelt's proclamation (which earned the moniker "midnight forests") meant that the forestry chief and his staff would now preside over more than 172 million acres of land. And while his young foresters took on the formidable task of managing those lands in the field, there were also forestry research initiatives to support. Early Forest Service employee Thornton Munger would later write to Pinchot that "it is an evidence of vision, progressiveness, and scientific spirit of the Forest Service that even under the pressure to take over the administration of a tremendous acreage of almost unknown and undeveloped public forests with a ridiculously small crew of very young men, research was not neglected. Coincident with the pressing problems of manning, developing, and protecting the national forests, studies were carried on of growth and yield, silvical characteristics of the important species, and methods of reforestation."[25]

The esprit de corps created by Pinchot and his lieutenants in Washington was the common subject of newspaper accounts (the Forest Service's in-house press bureau was highly effective in issuing releases and reports). A 1909 article in the *Denver Republican* captures the tenor of the times:

> *There's something characteristic in the head men of the forest service as if they had been inoculated with the Roosevelt-Pinchot virus; they are enthusiasts, every one of them. They give the impression that they are working for the love of forests—nature lovers bent on a great cause. Mr. Pinchot has enthusiasm to a degree, but more than that he can spread the contagion. In this respect the service is distinct. It keeps free from the taint of bureaucracy in its dealings with the public. The people are taken into the confidence of the chiefs.*[26]

As Gifford Pinchot was fashioning the Forest Service to be "the best Government organization of its day,"[27] another political storm brewing in California was about to force the chief to choose sides. The fallout would raise serious questions about the roles of preservation and conservation and the meaning of "the greatest good for the greatest number of people over the long haul" in ways that still resonate today.

CHAPTER SIXTEEN

Hetch Hetchy

GIFFORD PINCHOT FIRST MET JOHN MUIR ON JULY 16, 1896. MUIR, who had founded the Sierra Club four years prior and had gained national prominence for his writings on nature and the need to establish and protect Yosemite as a national park, joined the Forestry Commission's reconnaissance of western lands as they passed through Montana. Pinchot recalled his delight in meeting the celebrated naturalist, writer, and adventurer. "In his late fifties, tall, thin, cordial, and a most fascinating talker, I took to him at once," wrote Pinchot.[1]

Muir traveled with the members of the commission for several weeks as they visited the Bitterroot Mountains, Crater Lake, the Sierras, the San Bernardino Mountains, and the "San Jacintos," south of Los Angeles. How much time Pinchot and Muir had to discuss the splendor they witnessed or their philosophical views regarding nature or federal lands wasn't captured for posterity. What is known is that the two spent an "unforgettable day" on the rim of the Grand Canyon (which also became an impromptu overnight) while the other members of the party traveled to a scenic viewpoint and back. Pinchot reported that Muir was a "storyteller in a million" who entertained Pinchot with campfire tales until midnight."[2]

In 1899, Pinchot met Muir again. This time they were joined by the head of the Biological Survey, Hart Merriam, to see the Calaveras Grove of Sequoias. Then the head of the Division of Forestry, Pinchot's purpose in visiting was twofold: to learn more about the "growth and reproduction" of the "grandest of living things" and to issue a report to the Senate Committee on Public Lands making the case for protecting the giant trees by adding them to the Forest Reserves. (The first giant sequoia had been felled in 1853, only to be followed by thousands more. The Kings River Lumber Company alone felled eight thousand giant sequoias on a thirty-thousand-acre parcel.[3]) In the preservation of the one-thousand-plus-year-old wonders, Pinchot and Muir found common ground. But it would not happen again.

The issue that would drive Pinchot and Muir apart would henceforth redefine the meanings of conservation and preservation in American life. It would force a national conversation about the role of public lands. It would force public officials and private citizens to choose sides. And it would ultimately make the creation and protection of wilderness areas a part of that conversation. The issue was a proposed dam in Yosemite called Hetch Hetchy.

In 1882, city of San Francisco engineers presented the idea of building a dam in Yosemite's Hetch Hetchy Valley. The resulting reservoir, they promised, would be a source of both drinking water and hydro-electric power. The plan seemed to be defeated in 1890 when Yosemite became a national park. Between the turn of the century and 1905, the city of San Francisco tried three times to acquire water rights to the valley but were rebuffed by the Department of the Interior. The 1906 San Francisco earthquake was powerful enough to change the conversation. The need to provide the citizens of the city with an adequate water supply became enough of a cause to earn the backing of influential politicians and government officials. It is no surprise that Gifford Pinchot, who consistently advocated for "the greatest good for the greatest number of people" would support the dam building project.

As he testified to the House Committee on Public Lands in 1913, Pinchot summed up his point of view:

If there is, as the engineers tell us, no other source of supply that is anything like so reasonably available as this one; if this is the best, and, within reasonable limits of cost, the only means of supplying San

Francisco with water, we come straight to the question of whether the advantage of leaving this valley in a state of nature is greater than the advantage of using it for the benefit of the city of San Francisco.

The fundamental principle of the whole conservation policy is that of use, to take every part of the land and its resources and put it to that use in which it will best serve the most people, and I think there can be no question at all but that in this case we have an instance in which all weighty considerations demand the passage of the bill.[4]

Countering Pinchot's position at the hearing was John Muir's close friend Robert Underwood Johnson. In an impassioned speech, he told committee members that the nation was at an inflection point that imperiled both the sanctity of federal lands and people's faith in Congress itself.

There is something deeper in this matter than the question of whether you are going to destroy the great valley; whether you are going to turn in your tracks in this matter of conservation; whether you are going to expose all the national parks to invasion on similar pretexts, and, as I say, that is the fundamental question. This is a crisis. It is a fundamental question in the minds of the people whether they can trust the Congress of the United States and the Senate of the United States when a matter of commercialism comes into contact with the higher interests of the people.[5]

The years leading up to the final vote were contentious and spilled out of the halls of Congress and onto the printed page. Muir and Pinchot took the fight for public opinion to the pages of newspapers and magazines and privately to the president himself. The positions of the two men were clear: "Pinchot's ultimate loyalty was to civilization and forestry; Muir's was to wilderness and preservation."[6]

Muir's lobbying efforts included taking Roosevelt on a multiday camping and hiking tour of Yosemite in 1903. In one sense, the effort was a grand success. The combination of nature's grandeur and Muir's passion for the place had convinced Roosevelt that Yosemite Valley and

President Roosevelt and John Muir on their 1906 trip through Yosemite. (Library of Congress)

the Mariposa Big Tree Grove were worthy of being added to Yosemite National Park, an act he signed into law in June 1906.

But when it came to the fate of Hetch Hetchy, Gifford Pinchot's influence was even greater. Never wavering from his pragmatic "greatest good" principle, he won Roosevelt over. From the Sierra Club's point of view, "Pinchot's position was probably the decisive element in the administration's support of San Francisco."[7]

When President Wilson took office in March 1913, the Hetch Hetchy debate moved quickly toward resolution. With the president's appointment of former city attorney for San Francisco Franklin K. Lane as secretary of the interior, the Sierra Club and its allies knew they were in for a renewed fight. (Lane would later let it be known that he wasn't chosen for the job because of his ability to run the Interior Department but "because he could pull off the Hetch Hetchy deal."[8]) It took less than one week for the new secretary to declare that he would support the city in Congress.

In September 1913, the House of Representatives voted in favor of the Hetch Hetchy dam, and the Senate followed suit in December, passing the law by a 43–25 vote with 29 abstentions. Those who believed that the sanctity of national parks would forever be imperiled were mortified.

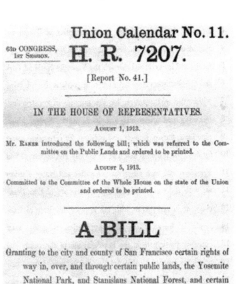

Introduced by Congressman John Raker (D-CA), the "Raker Bill" granted San Francisco the right to build the Hetch Hetchy dam. (National Archives)

Union Calendar No. 11.

63d CONGRESS,
1st Session.

H. R. 7207.

[Report No. 41.]

IN THE HOUSE OF REPRESENTATIVES.

August 1, 1913.

Mr. Raker introduced the following bill; which was referred to the Committee on the Public Lands and ordered to be printed.

August 5, 1913.

Committed to the Committee of the Whole House on the state of the Union and ordered to be printed.

A BILL

Granting to the city and county of San Francisco certain rights of way in, over, and through certain public lands, the Yosemite National Park, and Stanislaus National Forest, and certain lands in the Yosemite National Park, the Stanislaus National Forest, and the public lands in the State of California, and for other purposes.

1 Be it enacted by the Senate and House of Representa-
2 tives of the United States of America in Congress assembled,
3 That there is hereby granted to the city and county of San
4 Francisco, a municipal corporation in the State of California,
5 all necessary rights of way along such locations and of such
6 width, not to exceed two hundred and fifty feet, as in the

What was the use of creating a national park to protect it in perpetuity when the decision could be reversed by, as Muir put it, "devotees of raging commercialism . . . [who], instead of lifting their eyes to the God of the mountains, lift them to the almighty dollar"?[9]

The Hetch Hetchy debate had tested Gifford Pinchot's "greatest good" principle, and he had sided with the water and power companies, believing that it was right to "to take every part of the land and its resources and put it to that use in which it will best serve the most people."[10] That reasoning infuriated preservationists like Muir and Robert Underwood Johnson, who believed that the greatest good was protecting wild lands from damage that could not be undone. Said Johnson, "This is commercialism pure and simple, and the far-reaching results of this disposition of the national parks when the destruction of their supreme features is involved, is something appalling to contemplate."[11]

The conservation versus preservation debate hardly ended on the floor of the U.S. Senate in 1913. Indeed, it gave questions about the meaning and role of wilderness national and eternal standing. Historian Roderick Nash, author of *Wilderness and the American Mind*, wrote that "the principle of preserving wilderness was put to the test. For the first time in the American experience, the competing claims of wilderness and civilization to a specific area received a thorough hearing before a national audience."[12]

But even in losing that hearing, the preservationists had accomplished something remarkable. John Muir recognized as much, writing to Robert Underwood Johnson that "the conscience of the whole country has been aroused from sleep."[13] Indeed, their multiyear publicity and lobbying campaign had established that the appreciation for unspoiled nature and the need to preserve it was important to a significant number of Americans. In doing so, they created the first stirrings of a wilderness movement.

CHAPTER SEVENTEEN

The Chief Is Dismissed

WHEN THEODORE ROOSEVELT LEFT OFFICE ON MARCH 4, 1909, THE conservation movement's most powerful proponent was no longer in charge. If there was any hope that Roosevelt's conservation policies would remain intact, they were short lived. The newly elected President Taft immediately began reversing course. Not surprisingly, Pinchot, whose loyalty to both conservation and Roosevelt were absolute, would later remark (in reference to Taft's ascendency from cabinet officer to commander in chief) that "Taft, like many another failure in high places, was an admirable lieutenant, but a poor captain." Even worse, he felt, was his record on conservation. Decades later, Taft's dismantling of conservation policies would earn a blistering rebuke in Pinchot's autobiography, where he wrote,

> *The stand [Taft] deliberately assumed was water on the wheel of every predatory interest seeking to gobble up natural resources or otherwise oppress the people. It made him the accomplice and refuge of land grabbers, water-power grabbers, grabbers of timber and oil—all the swarm of big and little thieves and near-thieves, who, inside or outside of the law, were doing everything they knew to get possession of natural resources which belonged to the people and should have been conserved in the public interest.*[1]

However, it wouldn't take decades for fundamental philosophical differences in conservation policy to drive the men apart. The rift that developed between Pinchot and Taft would happen in real time, costing the nation's forester his job and, eventually, the chief executive his presidency.

THE BALLINGER-PINCHOT CONTROVERSY

In 1907, when Roosevelt was still president, his then secretary of the interior, James R. Garfield, chose an old college mate of his to serve as commissioner of the General Land Office. His old college chum's name was Richard Ballinger, a Seattle attorney who had once served as that city's mayor.

In Seattle, Ballinger had been legal counsel for Clarence Cunningham, a land speculator of questionable repute. Cunningham had orchestrated the acquisition of thirty-three 160-acre parcels in Alaska's Bering River coalfield. Although the law required that the owner could only lay claim to one parcel "for his own benefit, and not directly or indirectly, in whole or in part, in behalf of any person or persons whatsoever"[2] and that land claims could not be consolidated, Cunningham did not comply. Instead, he laid claim to the

Secretary of the Interior Richard Ballinger (shown in his office in 1909) became Gifford Pinchot's nemesis in the public scandal that would cost Pinchot his job. (Library of Congress)

parcels largely using aliases, then replaced with the names of friends and other associates who attached themselves to the scheme.

Two years before Ballinger's appointment, special agents in the federal Land Office (including one named Louis R. Glavis, who would become central to the tale) determined that Cunningham's claims were likely fraudulent and urged further investigation. Just one month after a determination was made to investigate Cunningham's activities, the thirty-three parcels were optioned to a conglomerate owned by J. P. Morgan & Company, the Guggenheim-owned American Smelting and Refining Company, and New York banking firms.[3]

Shortly after the options were signed transferring the claimed parcels to the powerful conglomerate, Ballinger called off the investigation. Seeking to put an end to the saga, he then drafted legislation that would validate the Cunningham claims and hand the Morgan-Guggenheim syndicate a great victory.

But Ballinger hit a roadblock. His boss, Secretary of the Interior Garfield, was against the bill, and so was Congress. A few months later, Ballinger handed Garfield a letter of resignation and headed back to Seattle to practice law. That might have been the end of the story, but fate had other plans.

Just one year after he had resigned his government post (and resumed his duties as an attorney representing Clarence Cunningham and friends), Ballinger was appointed by newly elected President Taft to be the new secretary of the interior. It was one of many early signals by Taft that he would undermine Roosevelt's (and Pinchot's) conservation efforts. (Another was the National Conservation Commission, to which Taft offered mild support and Congress allowed to die.) Noted Pinchot, "The Conservation movement had grown from a series of disjointed efforts into the most vital single public question before the American people. It had been planted and watered, and was just ready to blossom and bear fruit. But it was still too young to be safe."[4]

Land Office special agent Louis Glavis, already convinced that the Cunningham claims (and therefore the subsequent Morgan-Guggenheim claims) were obtained by fraudulent means, reported what transpired after Ballinger's installation at secretary of the interior in an article he penned for *Collier's* magazine:

> *Soon after he became Secretary of the Interior [Ballinger's] office rendered a decision which would have validated all fraudulent Alaska claims. A reversal of that decision on every point was obtained from Attorney-General Wickersham. Had it not been for Mr. Wickersham's decision, every fraudulent Alaska claim would have come to patent. I assert that in the spring of 1909 the Land Office urged me to an early trial of these cases before the investigation was finished, and when Secretary Ballinger, as the President has stated, knew that the Cun-*

ningham claims were invalid. When I appealed to Secretary Ballinger for postponement, he referred me to his subordinates. The Department of Agriculture intervened.[5]

The intervention was the result of a Glavis visit to Gifford Pinchot, who felt that "the natural resources of Alaska were in danger of monopoly" and that the fraud perpetuated by Cunningham and Ballinger needed to be stopped.[6] Glavis's visit was timely, because Pinchot had recently found out that all thirty-three of the disputed claims were within Alaska's Chugach National Forest, providing even greater incentive for him to jump into the fray. Pinchot gave Glavis a letter of introduction to Taft proposing a private meeting between the two men so the special agent could present his findings. At the same time, Pinchot wrote a personal letter to Taft emphasizing the importance of avoiding a public scandal and upholding the good name of the Taft administration. Finally, Pinchot dispatched a Forest Service lawyer to Chicago to meet Glavis and help prepare his report for the proposed Taft meeting.

A satirical cartoon of the time indicates that the Alaska land and coal claim scandal caused quite a stir. (Cornell University, PJ Mode Collection of Persuasive Cartography)

On August 18, 1909, Glavis presented his findings in person to President Taft along with his fifty-page report. Three weeks later, Ballinger presented his case to the president accompanied by an assistant and a one-thousand-plus-page report, which Taft claimed to have read and digested in just one night. The next day, he announced that Ballinger's actions were above reproach and, furthermore, that the secretary of interior had the authority to fire Glavis for insubordination.

Anticipating Pinchot's dismay, Taft wrote a letter asking the chief to stay in his post. He did so, less to appease Taft and more as an expression of loyalty to the former president and the retention of the conservation policies Pinchot and Roosevelt had put in place. Through a series of letters and personal meetings, the president and the forester defined the terms of their working relationship moving forward. Pinchot made it clear that he would continue to defend and promote conservation policies created for the benefit of America's citizens. Taft responded by attempting to assure Pinchot that Secretary Ballinger would "support the Government's policy of conserving natural resources" and asking him to refrain from creating further conflicts between departments by publishing articles critical of agencies and their officers in the press.[7]

The agreement didn't prevent Pinchot from making speeches critical of Ballinger and of policies that resulted in awarding natural resources to the monied few, even while freely acknowledging that such commentary might lead to his eventual firing. But the appearance of Glavis's article in *Collier's* was the catalyst that sped things along. Immediately after the article appeared, Ballinger filed a $1 million libel lawsuit against the publication (which hired Louis D. Brandeis as lead counsel). One month later, on December 21, 1909, a Senate resolution launched a congressional investigation of the Ballinger-Pinchot controversy.

Six days later, on December 27, Pinchot gave a speech. It would be his last as the nation's head forester. A blizzard prevented him from presenting his remarks to the intended audience in New Rochelle, New York (although he sent copies of his speech to various newspapers). Instead, he delivered his in-person remarks to "half a dozen friends in the University Club in New York." The speech is important in that it encapsulates the reasons why Pinchot continued to be steadfast in his defense of America's resources. He said, "The Conservation issue is a moral issue—that when a few men get possession of one of the necessities of life, and use that control to extort undue profits, they injure the average man without good reasons, and they are guilty of a moral wrong."[8]

The final cause for the chief's dismissal was that two of his inner circle (Overton W. Price and Alexander C. Shaw) had, unbeknownst to Pinchot, shared details about the Ballinger scandal with *Collier's*. Pinchot wrote a letter defending their actions to Senator Jonathan Dolliver of Iowa, who would in turn read it on the floor of the U.S. Senate. Asserting that the two were performing their duties as public officials, he wrote that Price and Shaw "were confronted by an extraordinary situation. Information had come to them which convinced them that the public interests in a manner within the line of their official duties were in grave danger at the hands of fraudulent claimants to these coal lands."[9]

The "Dolliver letter," as promised, was read in the Senate on January 6, 1910. The next day, Pinchot received a letter of termination written by President Taft. It was hardly a revelation to Pinchot, who'd been expecting the day to come since Taft's declarations of support for conservation began proving false. Trying to defend the Roosevelt-Pinchot vision of conservation with neither the support of other agencies nor the commander in chief had proven too difficult, largely because Pinchot didn't believe they were acting in good faith. Despite his stated intention to Taft that he would remain on the job "to defend the conservation politics whenever the need arises," the U.S. Forest Service's first leader's final act was to do what he thought best for the public interest even at the cost of leaving the job and people he loved.

On January 8, 1910, the day following his dismissal, Pinchot visited Forest Service headquarters to thank his colleagues. Reminding them that "the safe and decent handling of our timberlands is infinitely larger than any man's personal preference or personal fortunes," he urged them to stay on to work in the name of conservation. Behind the scenes, Pinchot successfully lobbied to have his longtime friend and colleague Henry Graves named as the new chief of the Forest Service, a post he would hold for the next decade.

When Gifford Pinchot left Washington, the agency he built was in good stead. His partnership with Roosevelt and ceaseless drive to prove that resources could and should be managed for the public good introduced the concept of conservation to millions of Americans. More important, he was able to present the management of the nation's national resources in terms of morality and equality—that federally protected forests, rivers, minerals, and grasslands belonged to all citizens, and they deserved to reap their benefits. The Ballinger-Pinchot controversy had provided the chief forester with the platform to drive that point home. Indeed, as one historian noted, "the publicity and dramatization that he gave to the controversy went far toward more firmly establishing conservation as a federal administrative program and a matter of fundamental public policy."[10]

The Ballinger-Pinchot controversy lingered long after Pinchot was fired and also changed the course of presidential history. Progressives were so disenchanted with Taft that Theodore Roosevelt formed the Progressive Party (aka the Bull Moose Party) after Roosevelt failed to secure the 1912 nomination for president. The resulting split vote enabled Woodrow Wilson to be elected to office.

CHAPTER EIGHTEEN

The National Forests Come East

THE WORK OF THE U.S. FOREST SERVICE HARDLY SLOWED DOWN AFTER its first boss left Washington and Henry Graves took the helm. In fact, a new initiative was taking place in the eastern states, one that aligned perfectly with young forester Benton MacKaye's background.

In 1911, Congress passed the Weeks Act, named after its sponsoring senator, John W. Weeks of Massachusetts. Prior to the passage of the act, all national forests had been carved out from lands already controlled by the federal government, the effect being that they only existed in western states. The Weeks Act was intended to facilitate the creation of eastern national forests. However, by the time the bill navigated its way through both chambers of Congress, there were several provisions attached—the most notable being that "the purchase of land for national forests were limited to land on the headwaters of navigable streams" and that all purchases would be vetted, approved, and negotiated by a specially created National Forest Reservation Commission comprised of two senators, two representatives, and the secretaries of the army, the interior, and agriculture.[1]

The inclusion of the "navigable streams" clause had been devised by a Forest Service attorney, Phillip P. Wells, as a means of appeasing opponents of the bill, such as "House Speaker Joe Cannon of Illinois, who vehemently opposed purchasing land with federal funds for what he considered purely scenic reasons."[2] The fiscally minded Speaker, upon recognizing that support for eastern forest reserves was on the rise, appointed House member John Weeks, a banker from Boston, to serve on the House Committee on Agriculture and, further, pledged his support for a forest bill if Weeks could draft one that would be acceptable to the business community. (A number of senators and their constituents still had a bad taste in their mouths regarding the size and number of forest reserves that had been created during Theodore Roosevelt's presidency and threatened "not only to block the legislation but [to] dismantle the Forest Service entirely and open up the national forests for private development."[3])

Given the political realities, Attorney Wells had determined (and Congressman Weeks subsequently agreed) that the interstate commerce clause of the U.S. Constitution granted the federal government the right to purchase forest watersheds to protect navigable rivers. The addition of that provision proved valuable enough to earn the eventual passage of the bill. It is important to note that the "navigable rivers" approach was not simply inserted as a legal trick for getting the Weeks Act passed. There was a legitimate business case for doing so.

In New Hampshire, where logging ran practically unchecked, hotel operators had raised their voices to protest the incessant threat of fires and the cleared-over landscapes despoiling the mountainsides. In an 1893 article, minister Julius H. Ward penned an article for the *Atlantic Monthly* stating that visitors who climbed to the summit of Mount Washington would see "what was once a magnificent wilderness, but where now the axe and fire have combined to leave what looks like a frightful desolation." He then added, "[It is] a frightful slaughter of the forest, the trees cut off entirely. . . . The youngest child of to-day will be gray or in his grave before this section is reafforested."[4]

But the scenery wasn't Ward's only concern. He and others had made the correlation between healthy forests and healthy watersheds. In the same article he wrote,

Where the trees grow thickly together, as the spruces and pines do, the soil beneath is porous, like a sponge, and soaks up a great deal of water from the showers and the melting snows, which trickles down into the streams drop by drop when the showers are over and the snows have disappeared. This sponginess of soil is not retained when the sunlight strikes through the foliage and dries it up. The rainfall may be the same, but the power of the soil to hold the water is impaired. Then again, if the woods are open, the ground freezes early, and when the heavy storms come, the water rushes down in torrents over this hard surface into the streams below and becomes a freshet. . . . It is in this light that the cutting of heavy timber in the White Mountain forests ought to be regarded.[5]

Ward's words proved prescient to a startling degree. The freshets of 1895 and 1896 were disastrous for New Hampshire's economy. In the autumn of 1896, the treasurer of the Amoskeag Cotton Mills in Manchester, New Hampshire, announced to stockholders that the flooding of the Merrimac River of the past two years had put six thousand of the company's employees out of work. Further, he attributed the flooding to the excessive cutting of forests surrounding the headwaters of the Merrimac and Pemigewasset Rivers and their tributaries. Treasurer Coolidge warned that if nothing was done, the water power of the Merrimac and their business would disappear. With that, he urged the immediate action by the next state legislature "to protect the forests still standing."[6]

Flooding wasn't only a threat to northeastern states. In March 1907, the heavily logged Monongahela River watersheds in West Virginia were buffeted by torrential rains. The resulting floods caused "over $100 million in damages before reaching Pittsburgh, where floods caused another $8 million in damages."[7]

The 1907 Pittsburgh flood drew attention to the need for forestry management. (University of Pittsburgh, Pittsburgh City Photographer Collection)

With the connection between forestry and commerce clearly established among business leaders and citizens living downstream, the inclusion of the "navigable rivers" clause in the Weeks Act attracted a more receptive audience.

To implement the act, the Forest Service would be charged with identifying forest tracts of interest and the Geological Survey with proving that such tracts in fact affected the navigability of nearby rivers. One of the first places the Forest Service and Geological Survey identified for potential acquisition was New Hampshire's White Mountains, and the man they hired to survey the region was Benton MacKaye.

The then thirty-three-year-old forester must have been thrilled to be plying his trade in the mountains he explored with Sturgis Pray back when he was blazing a trail through the Swift River Valley. Even more exciting to MacKaye may have been the prospect of helping to establish a national forest encompassing Zealand Notch and the Pemigewasset River valley, both of which had been logged by J. E. Henry & Sons, whose company had been responsible for an 1886 forest fire that consumed a seven-mile-long swath of trees[8] and whose namesake once vowed "not to leave any tree standing in the 'Pemi,' no matter how small or immature they were."[9]

It was the perfect job for MacKaye. Mostly alone from late summer through the onset of winter, he toted maps and surveying equipment through valleys and climbed to the headwaters of eight river basins, taking careful measure of forest cover, tree species, and stream flow and taking precise notes and slowly shaping them into what would become a watershed document in every sense of the phrase—one that made a scientific case for the establishment and protection of national forests. As MacKaye biographer Larry Anderson stated, "He had helped, in a modest way, to refine the discipline of scientific forestry in America, which had proceeded as much on faith and uplifting rhetoric as on empirically documented fact."[10]

MacKaye's work earned the praise of his superiors back in Washington, but the years of government service ahead would not provide either the solitude or the joys he experienced over those few months in the New England mountains. Increasingly he would discover that his ideals weren't quite aligned with those of his employers and vice versa. Mac-Kaye's grand ideas often contained brilliant, actionable aspects, but also parts that were too progressive to be embraced by his peers and bosses. It was as if his compass bearing was just a degree or two off from a career in forestry—the further he followed the avocation's path, the further he drifted away from a fulfilling existence.

As for the Weeks Act, it unequivocally accomplished its goal of establishing national forests in the states east of the Mississippi River. More than that, it made the national forests truly national and established the U.S. Forest Service as the "nation's forest service."[11]

From the first eleven purchases in 1912 (which included the lands that would become the White Mountain National Forest), the number of holdings grew, thanks in part to an amendment added in 1924 that added "timber production" as one of the purposes of land acquisition. By the fiftieth anniversary of the passage of the Weeks Act, it accounted for twenty-three million acres of new national forests, the majority of which were created east of the Great Plains. Notably, many of the lands acquired "were in poor condition because of excessive timber cutting, fire damage and erosion."[12] It is here we can find one of the greatest successes of the legislation and of forest management.

Weeks Act land purchases gave the [Forest Service] its first experience with landscape-scale restoration as foresters applied professional forest management practices to once neglected lands across the East. . . . After decades of reforestation efforts, these national forests now support abundant flora and fauna and hide most of the scars of past abuse.[13]

CHAPTER NINETEEN

Along Comes the National Park Service

BY 1914, AN ENORMOUS AMOUNT OF WORK HAD BEEN ACCOMPLISHED in the name of creating a national forest system encompassing hundreds of millions of acres of America's lands. What's more, due largely to the efforts of Gifford Pinchot, the agency had the staff of dedicated foresters, rangers, inspectors, and supervisors needed to manage the forests, grasslands, and mining activities on those lands. But there was another disparate set of federal lands in need of attention—the national parks and monuments.

The contentious Hetch Hetchy debate had brought into focus how tenuous the protection of the country's protected lands really was. If one dam could be constructed within a national park, preservationists wondered, what was to prevent any of them from being desecrated? One person asking that question as 1914 ended was a thirty-seven-year-old named Stephen Mather.

A San Francisco native who graduated from the University of California in 1887, Mather spent the first part of his professional career writing for the *New York Sun*, where he befriended a fellow journalist named Robert Sterling Yard, a partnership that would strengthen with time. Five years into his career, Mather left newspaper work to join the Pacific Coast Borax Company, where his father was an administrator. The younger Mather was put in charge of advertising and distribution of the product and was credited with creating the name "20 Mule Team Borax," which thrust the brand onto the national stage. In 1904, Mather partnered with a friend to create a competing Borax company, a venture that made him a millionaire and allowed him to turn his full attention to a cause that stirred his interest far more than running his Borax firm.

In 1904, Mather became a member of the Sierra Club. The following year, he joined the club's annual outing at Mount Rainier. There he met several of the club's luminaries and had ample time to learn about and discuss the pressing issues ahead of them, including the Hetch Hetchy threat. In 1912, Mather visited Yosemite and experienced one of the highlights of his life, "the opportunity to have a long talk with the legendary Muir, whose whole life at this time was fighting the Hetch Hetchy dam."[1] Muir also impressed on Mather the need to add lands to Sequoia National Park or perhaps create a new park between Yosemite and Sequoia. Not long after his trip to Yosemite, Mather made his way to Washington to attend the congressional hearings on Hetch Hetchy.

In 1913, Mather received a letter from an acquaintance he'd made at the hearings indicating that the Hetch Hetchy decision would be ruled in the city of San Francisco's favor. (It may be recalled that Secretary Lane had formerly served as city attorney for San Francisco, which put the man in charge of America's national parks in an interesting position.) However, Mather's connection (Robert Marshall of the U.S. Geological Survey and no relation to the forester of the same name whom we will soon meet) suggested in the same letter that the Sierra Club and others who fought for Hetch Hetchy use their accumulated influence to lobby for park expansion. Armed with maps supplied by Marshall, Mather hiked from Lake Tahoe to Mount Whitney in 1914. The trip further strengthened Mather's emerging view that the country needed a national park service.

ABOUT THAT LETTER

The popular story is that Stephen Mather wrote a letter to Interior Department secretary Franklin Lane (whom he was rumored to have known as a fellow student at UC Berkeley) in late 1914 "condemning the deteriorating conditions of the [National] Parks which suffered from logging, hunting, roaming cattle and other conditions."[2] Upon reading the letter, Lane allegedly responded with one of his own, writing, "Dear

Steve, if you don't like the way the parks are being run, come on down to Washington and run them yourself"—an offer Mather couldn't pass up.

It made for a great story, but it wasn't accurate. In reality, the two had never met before Mather penned his letter, and the circumstances of his hiring involved a period of due diligence by Lane and of soul searching by Mather.

According to Horace Albright, who was an administrator for Secretary Lane and went on to become Mather's more than able assistant, the initial meeting proceeded as follows:

> [Lane] stressed the fact that [the national parks] were orphans. They were split among three departments—War, Agriculture, and Interior. They were anybody's business and therefore nobody's business. The time was ripe for some person who really cared to wade into the problem, get them united in a strong, separate bureau, and get Americans acquainted with their own scenic and historic sites instead of spending their time and money in foreign countries. Lane made it clear that Mather's job would be to lobby Congress for a national parks bureau. Lane pointed out that he was hog-tied on that score for he was a "marked man" because of leading the fight for Hetch Hetchy.[3]

After thinking about it for a few weeks, Mather made a counteroffer to Secretary Lane in early January 1915. He'd accept the job and perform it for one year if he could have Horace Albright as his assistant. Mather was sworn into office on January 21, 1915. He stayed for fourteen years.

Mather's first inclination was to build grassroots support for the creation of a national parks bureau by getting more citizens to experience the parks firsthand. A combination of national publicity and increased visits might be enough to get Congress finally moving toward establishing a park service. But he'd need help, and he knew where to get it. Mather reached out to his old friend from his *New York Sun* days, Robert Sterling Yard, and brought him on as the department's publicity man.

Mather and Yard initiated their campaign by sending out a nearly endless stream of press releases and articles about America's national parks, urging fellow Americans to discover their wonders. The centerpiece of the campaign was Yard's brainchild—the *National Parks Portfolio*. Yard and Mather solicited photographs from various government agencies, the railroads, and individuals that showcased the national parks. Yard wrote the text, and Mather put up $5,000 of his own money to have the book prepared for printing. Mather then got the western railroads to chip in $40,000 to have 275,000 copies printed. The portfolios were distributed to libraries, travel agencies, outdoor clubs, garden clubs, every member of Congress, and other prominent Americans. (In 1916, Yard created a smaller edition titled *Glimpses of Our National Parks*. The 2.7 million copies were largely sold through the national parks and in bookstores.[4])

The publicity campaign was creating awareness and increasing visits to the parks, but Mather felt it was time to get influential business leaders and government officials involved in his drive to create a national parks bureau. What better place to do it, he thought, than in Yosemite, where, if he was lucky, he could also garner support for the addition of surrounding lands into the system?

Mather (and presumably Yard) invited a who's who of industrialists, journalists, naturalists, politicians, photographers, zoologists, engineers, and financiers—twenty people, plus two cooks, to saddle up and ride through the high country of the Sierras.

On July 21, 1915, the Mather party arrived at their Junction Meadow campsite ahead of schedule. After relaxing for much of the afternoon, Mather convinced his assistant, Horace Albright, and Gilbert Grosvenor (the first full-time employee and future director of the National Geographic Society, who had been hired in 1899 by then NGS president Alexander Graham Bell) to make a late afternoon hike up into Kern-Kaweah Canyon. Reaching a ridgeline notch at the top of their ascent, they were astounded by the view of the Kaweah Peaks beyond and the Rockslide Lakes below. Albright recalled,

> *I will always remember that day, that place, and the discussions we had. This part of the Sierra presented a whole new world to us. . . . We were silent and awestruck by the bold majesty of the vista. Then, almost in unison, we began an earnest discussion of what could be*

done to enclose the Kern, Kings and Whitney regions into an enlarged Sequoia or an entirely new park.[5]

As the trio sat looking over the incomparable vista, the discussion took on a wider perspective, one that embraced more than the acquisition and protection of the lands surrounding them, to encompass a vision for the future—one that for the first time was built on the assumption that a national parks bureau would come into being.

"That is why this day was so memorable," Albright said. "For each of us contributed ideas, but also the practical avenues to reach these goals. We remembered what we said that glorious afternoon when we returned to Washington."[6]

Thus began a considerable shift in Mather's thinking. Until now, he'd believed that the key to getting Congress behind the creation of a national parks bureau hinged on getting more people to visit the already established parks. But the expedition through the Sierras had led him to a different conclusion, "that the improvement of the parks and publicizing them would amount to little without the power of a formal, organized bureau in the Interior Department."[7]

Five days later, after the Mather Mountain Party had enjoyed one of their last meals under the Sierra stars, the leader stood up to say a few words. He began by telling the eighteen remaining team members that the time had come for him to confess why he had brought them together. It wasn't only for their interesting company, he admitted, but in the hopes that they

would see the significance of these mountains in the whole picture of what we are trying to do . . . that unless we protect the areas currently held [by establishing] a separate government agency, we may lose them to selfish interests. And we need this [new] bureau to enhance and enlarge our public lands, to preserve infinitely more, "for the benefit and enjoyment of the people" as the Yellowstone act stated.[8]

Mather concluded by asking everyone seated at the table to become evangelists for the national parks bureau movement—for business leaders to contact clubs, organizations, and friends interested in the outdoors, for political leaders to get after their colleagues to support legislation, and for representatives of state agencies to pledge support and cooperation. Remember, he said, "God has given us these beautiful lands. Try to save them for, and share them with, future generations. Go out and spread the gospel!"[9]

Gilbert Grosvenor was so moved by the experience and the possibilities for America's park movement that *National Geographic* dedicated an entire issue in 1916 to the national parks.[10] In terms of spreading the gospel, he had certainly done his part. And the American public soon followed suit.

Mather and Yard's publicity campaign was also having an effect in Washington. On August 25, 1916 (just nineteen months after Mather took up the cause), President Woodrow Wilson signed the act establishing the National Park Service (NPS) into law. The act specified that the newly formed National Park Service was established to promote and regulate national parks, monuments, and reservations "by such means and measures as conform to the fundamental purpose of [them—] to conserve the scenery and the natural and historic objects and the wild life therein and to provide for the enjoyment of the same in such manner and by such means as will leave them unimpaired for the enjoyment of future generations."[11]

The first challenges to implementing the new law were administrative. In the wake of the bill's signing, Mather retained his position as assistant secretary of the interior, brought Robert Marshall over from Geological Survey to become interim director of the NPS, named Horace Albright assistant director, and put Robert Sterling Yard in charge of the service's new educational division. Things got off to a rocky start.

Robert Marshall proved to be a poor administrator, whom Albright described as "tactless, stubborn, and quick to argue."[12] The final straw came when Marshall, fearing a railroad strike that might leave travelers stranded in Yellowstone, issued an order to close the park before the tourist season ended. Infuriated concessioners and politicians from Montana and Wyoming flooded Park Service headquarters with complaints, and Mather (with Lane's consent) had Marshall transferred back to the Geological Survey.

In January 1917, the second shoe dropped. In the midst of a multiday National Parks Conference, Stephen Mather suffered a debilitating mental breakdown, one that required nearly a year of convalescence followed by a slow assimilation back to work as the director of the National Park Service. The seriousness of Mather's condition was kept between Jane Mather, Secretary Lane, and Horace Albright ("Then the charade began of hiding Mather's true condition from the public eye," he recalled).

Despite the major disruptions in leadership, the national park idea took hold and then some. Between 1916 and 1921, the number of visitors rose from 365,000 to over 1 million.[13] It was clear Americans loved their parks. The greatest challenge in managing them soon emerged. It was a question that harkened back to Frederick Law Olmsted's Mariposa Report—how could you accommodate large numbers of visitors while retaining the grandeur of the surroundings that attracted them there in the first place? As the number of automobile owners traveling to parks and the need for roads to take them there increased, the question only became more difficult to answer.

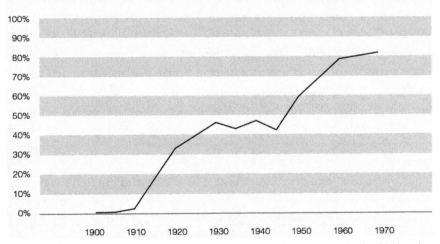

Percentage of car owning households in U.S.

The rise of automobile ownership introduced profound challenges to the National Park Service and raised questions about the relationship between cars and public lands. (Jim Cannon)

In 1921, the National Park Service was clearly in the road building and road improvement business. The agency requested $500,000 per year for five years to "construct necessary roads within the parks" and recommended that the federal government commit funds for building "feeder roads" to national park entrances. Declared Mather, "In my opinion the completion of this work will supply the country with a scenic highway comparable to none, and I predict that what now seem large travel figures will sink into insignificance before the stream of motorists who will then avail themselves of the opportunity and pleasure to visit the parks, with the freedom possible only by riding along in one's own car."[14]

A second initiative to promote car travel to national parks was the "Great Circle Highway." Developed by Mather in partnership with the National Park-to-Park Highway Association, the six-thousand-mile road facilitated travel between the great western parks. The route was showcased in the 1920 *Report of the Director of the National Park Service* (to Congress).

As automobile ownership and park visits continued to skyrocket, more facilities needed to be built within the parks—hotels, campgrounds, concession stands, roads, hiking trails, and parking lots among them. Outside park boundaries, more accommodations—gas stations, stores, restaurants, hotels, and more sprang up to take advantage of the tourist traffic.

Horace Albright noted that the arrival of the automobile on the scene affected the Park Service's mandate practically overnight. "We recognized that the introduction of automobiles would vastly increase visitation to the parks and their use," he said. "However, we also knew the Congress would count tourist visitation to decide how much our bureau would get to operate the park system. Dollars would be doled out according to the number of visitors."[15]

One person in the National Park Service whom the use/preservation paradox began eating at was Robert Sterling Yard, who increasingly viewed the infrastructure building within the parks as a threat to the parks themselves. As historian Paul Sutter brilliantly observed, Yard's "testaments to the sublime and majestic beauty of the parks, which had been potent ammunition in opposing resource development, had the opposite effect on tourist development."[16] Yard had so effectively advertised the parks that pieces of them were being chipped away to accommodate visitor traffic—so much so that he believed the very character of at least some of the parks had been compromised.

Yard had difficulty finding a receptive audience within the NPS for his growing criticism of the agency's trajectory. Stephen Mather was often unreachable due to either his need to travel or to recuperate, and Horace Albright (as noted) felt that the number of visitors and NPS funding were codependent—park improvements in the name of better visitor experiences were always welcome. Working in a separate building and serving as the editor of the National Parks Association publications (an arrangement Mather orchestrated in the early days so that he could pay Yard out of his own pocket) also put Yard at a disadvantage.

By the early 1930s, Robert Sterling Yard had wrestled with the conundrum long enough to realize that he was becoming an advocate for primitive, roadless areas—places to be preserved in the spirit of what created the national parks without the attendant push for tourism-related development. As such, he became aware of a growing chorus of like-minded people. When Yard was relieved of his post in 1933, he was ready to hear more.

CHAPTER TWENTY

MacKaye's Historic Path

WHEN BENTON MACKAYE WAS FORTY-TWO YEARS OLD, HE WAS SUDdenly faced with the second great tragedy of his life. While visiting a friend in Quebec, he received a telegram that his wife, Betty Stubbs MacKaye, was ill and that he should immediately come home. At that time in his life, "home" was a New York City apartment.

Betty MacKaye had battled depression most of her life. Past episodes of varying intensity had, until the current crisis, always been followed by better days. The darkest episode had necessitated a stay with her dear friend, a Universalist minister and lecturer named Mabel Irwin, who lived outside the city in Croton-on-Hudson, some forty miles north of their West Twelfth Street apartment. After evaluating the situation that called him home in April 1921, Benton decided that another trip to the facility was warranted. While waiting for a train at Penn Station, Betty broke away from Benton and Mrs. Irwin (who had come to the city to help chaperone Betty) and disappeared into the crowd. Searching proved futile. After employing the help of police without success, a distraught Benton MacKaye went home.

Soon he received word from the police that Betty MacKaye's body had been found floating in the East River, a victim of her own suicide. Benton was so shaken that he couldn't bring himself to identify Betty's body in the morgue. He asked Mrs. Irwin and his close friend Charles Harris Whitaker to go on his behalf.

After spending some time at his brother's house, MacKaye received a letter from Whitaker, inviting him to his farmstead in Mount Olive,

New Jersey. By summer, Benton was finding solace in writing. He drafted a thorough "Memorandum on Regional Planning"—"a far-reaching plan for the transformation of modern American industrial society that emphasized play as a first priority."[1] While several aspects of MacKaye's manifesto interested his host, who was not only a confidant but also the editor of the *Journal of the American Institute of Architects*, Whitaker immediately grasped the profound possibilities for pairing community planning and recreation. He suggested that MacKaye revise his work to focus on that aspect of his proposal.

Harkening back to his explorations with Sturgis Pray and Horace Hildreth, MacKaye envisioned creating a footpath from New Hampshire's Mount Washington to North Carolina's Mount Mitchell. The trail would offer recreational escape for citizens who were increasingly discovering the restorative power of being in nature (as MacKaye himself had experienced, most notably in the wake of two personal tragedies). But the trail would also encourage an exodus for people who were dissatisfied with city life and provide significant economic benefits to rural areas that had lost significant numbers of people to urban flight. In historian Paul Sutter's view, "MacKaye saw recreation and recuperation as preliminary to and complementary with what he hoped would be a reorientation in American economic culture, back toward nature and a direct working relationship with the land. Such resettlement, he hoped, would arise from recreation."[2]

If visitors found enjoyment from recreating in the outdoors, reasoned MacKaye, perhaps they would make the leap to move to the country where they could "work in the open" as well. This transformation would be encouraged because being on the trail would allow periods of reflection, something MacKaye had experienced on his own rambles in the mountains. (His soul-stirring experience on top of Mount Tremont comes to mind.) He believed that similar experiences would inspire visitors to question the rise of industrialization and their role as workers.

Life for two weeks on the mountain top would show up many things about life during the other fifty weeks down below. The latter could

be viewed as a whole—away from its heat, sweat, and irritations.
There would be a chance to catch a breath, to study the dynamic forces
of nature and the possibilities of shifting to them the burdens now
carried on the backs of men. The reposeful study of these forces should
provide a broad gauged enlightened approach to the problems of
industry. Industry would come to be seen in its true perspective—as a
means in life and not an end in itself.[3]

Yet, MacKaye emphasized, the Appalachian Trail would not just be
created for the benefit of those who spent days and weeks on the mountaintops. It would be the centerpiece of an economic engine, employing
some forty thousand people to build the trail, developing lasting "opportunities—for recreation, recuperation and employment—in the region of
the Appalachian skyline" and to "establish a base for a more extensive and
systematic development of outdoor community life."[4]

On July 10, 1921, Benton MacKaye and his host, Charles Harris
Whitaker, presented MacKaye's plan for "An Appalachian Trail" to
Clarence Stein, chairman of the Committee on Community Planning
for the American Institute of Architects. The trio met at a recreational
retreat known as Hudson Guild Farm. Before the meeting concluded,
Whitaker agreed to publish an article in the AIA journal, and Stein,
a key figure in what would be known as the Garden City movement,
agreed to promote the trail.

Published in October 1921 under the headline "An Appalachian
Trail: A Project in Regional Planning," the idea for the "AT" quickly
gained speed. Columnist Raymond Torrey of the *New York Evening
Post* provided a significant boost on April 7, 1922, with his article, "A
Great Trail from Maine to Georgia," complete with an early map styled
after the one MacKaye had originally provided with his AIA article.
Torrey also helped build the first miles of the AT in the Bear Mountain
area of New York.

After some initial fits and starts, the Appalachian Trail gained
permanent momentum in 1929 when twenty-nine-year-old Myron
Avery took the project's helm. By 1937, he had succeeded in scouting

the footpath (he walked most of the two thousand plus miles himself), writing the guidebooks, overseeing the production of maps, founding most of the trail clubs that built and maintained the trails, and garnering publicity for it. He had also succeeded in pushing Benton MacKaye to the sidelines (which was helped along by MacKaye's relative introversion and his constant need to eke out a living). Things may have worked out fine between the men if it weren't for two fundamental differences—approach and style.

In a word, Myron Avery was "caustic." He was prone to tossing aside people who didn't agree with him and engaging in controversies to support his singular agenda of building an uninterrupted trail from Georgia to Maine. It can be argued, with merit, that without that focus, the trail would never have been completed. But Avery's "take no prisoners" approach also alienated many people, most significantly Benton MacKaye.

Their differences simmered then came to a full boil in 1934. At issue was the creation of Skyline Drive in Shenandoah National Park, an undertaking set in motion by President Hoover in the fall of 1930 and pursued with great zeal by the National Park Service. In only two years, the first thirty-four miles of the ridgetop highway had been constructed, obliterating sections of the Appalachian Trail and, most concerning to Benton MacKaye, defiling the mountaintops, destroying the wilderness character and its ability to hold the problems associated with work life and industrialism at bay. His idea was, in fact, being paved over.

After initially siding with MacKaye in expressing dismay to the National Park Service, Myron Avery came to favor coexistence. His desire to have a contiguous trail, even if it needed to run alongside a paved road, would continue to be his objective. By 1934, the always tenuous working relationship between founder MacKaye and builder Avery was deteriorating with increasing speed.

Avery was frustrated by MacKaye's entreaties to the NPS and floor proposals at Appalachian Trail Conference meetings by MacKaye for the ATC to formally oppose skyline drives (which were proposed for Vermont, New Hampshire, Virginia, Pennsylvania, and Georgia). At the Southern Appalachian Trail Conference held in May 1934, Avery (who did not attend but sent a statement) minimized the issue, saying that the priority should be completing the trail first, then entertaining questions regarding how to use it. Predictably, MacKaye (who *was* in attendance) stated the opposite. "A wilderness is like a secret. The best way to keep it is to *keep* it. Keep the wilderness *wild*."[5] MacKaye's appeal was mildly successful in that the conference adopted a resolution that the "crestline or skyline" of the trail be "preserved exclusively for primitive recreation via foot paths where desirable"[6]—hardly the forceful declaration MacKaye was after.

MacKaye hoped for better luck at the Sixth Annual Appalachian Trail Conference, which was held the following month in Rutland, Vermont. He had reason to be optimistic. The citizens of Vermont were embroiled in a parkway controversy of their own. The proposed Green Mountain Parkway would travel "the length of Vermont, following the spine of the Green Mountains, passing near the top of every major peak in the state, including Killington, Pico, Camel's Hump, Mansfield and Jay."[7] MacKaye naturally believed he would find support among those who would be most affected by skyline drives, the hiking community itself. The Green Mountain Club had publicly come out against the project because it would destroy much of the existing Long Trail (the predecessor to the AT, which extended the length of the state along the crest of the Green Mountains and shared its southernmost one hundred miles with the AT).

Interestingly, proponents of the project had reached out to Frederick Law Olmsted Jr. (who had followed in his father's footsteps to head the family firm) for support but found it lacking. In a letter to the project's champion, James Paddock Taylor, Olmsted Jr. stated that although he didn't have enough familiarity with the region to offer a "confident and thoroughly well-grounded opinion," he still considered the greenway to be "of very doubtful expediency and possibly very wasteful and unwise," an opinion that proponents understandably kept to themselves.[8]

But proponents found a more compelling reason to push the Green Mountain Parkway—economics. In the 1930s (as today), Vermont's economy relied heavily on tourism. The parkway would greatly improve access to the Green Mountain State and prosperity at a time when its citizens needed it most. "Moreover . . . the parkway would open Vermont and Vermonters to a wider world and break through Vermont's reputation as isolated and provincial."[9]

That argument hit home hard enough to weaken the Green Mountain Club's official stance on the project. Many of the same members who relished the advantages of being in the outdoors also relied on the tourism dollars of those who visited the area for the same reasons. By the time Benton MacKaye's proposal for the ATC to officially oppose skyline drives came to the conference floor in June 1934, he could no longer rely on full-throated support.

In March 1934, MacKaye had articulated his objections to skyline drives and offered an alternative in a piece he wrote for *Appalachia* titled "Flankline vs. Skyline." The issue of "skyline motor roads," he wrote, "involves the fate of the Appalachian wilderness as our hinterland of outdoor recreation." With sides so deeply entrenched, he offered a solution for satisfying "such apparently divergent desires for scenery and solitude."[10] MacKaye's premise was that motorists would enjoy a better driving experience, one "that brings out the close-up landscape and sets forth the range in all its angles . . . from base to timberline" yet also "leaves the wilderness intact."[11]

Flankline vs. Skyline

By Benton MacKaye[1]

PROPOSALS have recently been made for crowning certain of the Appalachian ranges with skyline motor roads, including the Presidential Range, the Green Mountains, the Blue Ridge, and the Great Smokies. This is an issue indeed: it involves the fate of the Appalachian wilderness as our hinterland of outdoor recreation. One group is for the roads, the other against them. How can we satisfy such apparently divergent desires for scenery and solitude?

MacKaye's introduction to his article in *Appalachia* magazine immediately pointed to the challenges of finding common ground. (Courtesy of *Appalachia*)

The piece, written at the request of the journal's editors, was intended to "explain and enforce the point of view which the A.M.C. and other similar organizations have adopted on the question of skyline motor roads." An editor's footnote to the article additionally stated that "the strength of Mr. MacKaye's position, and the special value of his article, lie in the fact that he is not a mere opponent of such roads but is able to offer an alternative suggestion which would even better serve the purposes of the motorist while not spoiling the mountains for the tramper."[12]

Three months after the publication of MacKaye's article, his proposal for the Appalachian Trail Conference to stand unequivocally opposed to the skyline drives and for the organization to do everything in its power to ensure "that whatever highways or parkways are built near the Appalachian Ranges be located along the lower flanks and levels"[13] came to the floor. It fell flat. Even if MacKaye had been in attendance,* the proposal's passage would have been in doubt. Ironically, the state of Vermont's road planners had recently introduced the idea of a flank-line route. At least some conference attendees indicated that because the alternative route was being proposed, they could not stand behind MacKaye's proposal for fear of the ATC being branded as opposed to mountain parkways regardless of their location.

Once again, MacKaye's proposal would not win the day. It was pulled from consideration, and the Appalachian Trail Conference proceeded with other business. But neither MacKaye nor Avery was satisfied with the result. MacKaye felt that the proposals to build skyline drives across the mountaintops were an immediate threat to the trail as he envisioned it. The trail is "no end in itself," he stated, rebutting the assertion Avery commonly made; rather, it was conceived "as a means of sojourning in the primeval or wilderness environment whose preservation and nurture is your particular care."[14] Further, the skyline drive craze (or "scheme," as MacKaye was prone to call it) was a threat to society's collective well-being, "the possibilities for health and recuperation," and "the means for

---

*It is interesting to note that MacKaye and Avery were not both at the Southern Appalachian Trail Conference (which MacKaye attended) and the ATC Conference (which Avery attended). With tensions running high about the skyline roads debate, it is easy to speculate that one or both situations were planned avoidances.

escaping the grinding-down process of our modern life."[15] It was too vital an issue to simply drop.

However, Myron Avery was an equally determined foe, who felt that MacKaye's proposals were preventing the ATC from doing its important work of completing the trail from Georgia to Maine, regardless of where the path needed to be built. After the 1934 conference, while Benton MacKaye pondered his next steps, Avery laid the groundwork to diminish MacKaye's influence and ability to raise the issue again. One year later, Avery's plan went into effect in a manner consistent with his contentious personality.

Before the 1935 Appalachian Trail Conference, Avery leveraged the relationships he had built during the six years he presided over the organization. Nothing had been done in those years without Avery's blessing (he even went so far as to choose the paint used to mark the trail). Many of the trail's caretaking clubs had been founded by Avery, with board officers hand-selected by him. Thus he was in position to ensure that any 1935 proposal for the ATC to formally oppose roads would fail.

When MacKaye's friends Harold Anderson (the Potomac Appalachian Trail Club secretary who had been on the memorable visit to Skyline Drive also attended by MacKaye and Avery), Raymond Torrey (the columnist for the *Post* who introduced the AT to the world at large), and two other attendees submitted a resolution for the ATC to formally oppose skyline drives at the 1935 conference, Avery countered with his preplanned alternative, a proposal that any projects that potentially interfered with the AT would be weighed on their own merits and, further, that if the project was a skyline drive, the ATC would encourage the federal agency involved (likely the NPS) to rebuild the trail in an alternate location.

If MacKaye's loyalists weren't already offended, they only needed to wait for the other shoe to drop. Avery had prepared nominations for board members and amendments to the ATC's constitution that included apportioning the voting power of various trail clubs based on the mileage each was responsible for overseeing. The passage of those amendments gave Avery complete and official control over the organization's charter and operations. Torrey, Anderson, and others resigned in protest before the conference was over.

In the aftermath, the man who had conceived the Appalachian Trail was no longer welcome in the organization created to build and protect it. Even more discouraging to MacKaye and his followers was the fact that Myron Avery and the ATC attendees "were not ready to sacrifice the possibility of a continuous trail for the principle of undefiled wilderness."[16]

Benton MacKaye may not have foreseen the events that pulled the rug out from under him, but he was prepared for them. Because just after the 1934 Appalachian Trail Conference, Harold Anderson, MacKaye, and like-minded colleagues founded an "organization of spirited people who [would] fight for the freedom of the wilderness."[17]

CHAPTER TWENTY-ONE

Voices for the Wilderness

BY THE MID-1920S, SEPARATE VOICES ADVOCATING FOR THE ESTABLISH-
ment of primitive "roadless" areas were beginning to gain audiences—
sometimes with success.

THE WORLD'S FIRST WILDERNESS AREA

The first wilderness area breakthrough was made by a young forester who,
like many in the profession, had attended the Yale Forestry School and
been hired by Gifford Pinchot. But Aldo Leopold would be destined to
leave his significant mark not only in forestry, but conservation, philosophy, education, and literature.*

Leopold was born and raised in Burlington, Iowa, in a home overlooking the Mississippi River. His father was an avid hunter, fisherman, and
early conservationist who introduced Aldo to the "moral responsibility for
their sustaining of the natural world."[1] In an era when "market hunting"
(taking indiscriminate amounts of fish and game) was common because
supplies were deemed infinite, father Carl taught his son that such practices were unethical and urged him to consider the resource as a whole—
lessons that were absorbed and shared by Aldo throughout his life.

---

*Aldo Leopold's contribution to the fields of conservation, game management, and watershed
management and his perspectives on our relationship with the land and our ethical responsibility to
"treat land as a community to which we belong" covers far more ground than can be covered in the
context of this book. For a deeper dive, I suggest reading Curt Meine's biography, *Aldo Leopold: His
Life and Work* and/or Leopold's groundbreaking conservation book, *A Sand County Almanac.* A video
documentary of his life can be seen at www.VoicesoftheWilderness.com.

Aldo Leopold working for the U.S. Forest Service in New Mexico in 1911. (Courtesy of the Aldo Leopold Foundation and the University of Wisconsin–Madison archives)

Aldo Leopold spent nearly fifteen years working for the U.S. Forest Service, two in Arizona and thirteen in New Mexico. During those years he became convinced that some pieces of wild land should simply be left alone. In 1921 Leopold lobbied his supervisors to create a continuous stretch of country preserved in its natural state. In a memo he wrote around the time he proposed the wilderness area, he sought to further clarify his meaning of the term "wilderness" as "an area publicly owned and permanently dedicated to public use for some distinctive form of outdoor recreation or study requiring primitive means of subsistence and travel in a wild environment."[2]

Three years after submitting his plan, as Leopold was embarking on a new phase of his career working for the Forest Products Laboratory in Wisconsin, he got word that his wilderness proposal had been accepted. The Forest Service set aside 750,000 acres of desert, rivers, and mountains in New Mexico as the Gila Wilderness. It was the first area in the world to be designated and protected as a wilderness, and it set the stage for the broader acceptance of a wilderness movement.

A LIFELONG CAUSE IN MINNESOTA

In 1925, the year after Leopold's vision for creating a wilderness area was achieved, local citizens of the Rainy Lake area, adjacent to International Falls, Minnesota, started hearing rumors about a massive dam building project proposed for their community by lumber baron Edward Wellington Backus. His seven-dam project would "turn much of the watershed into a hydroelectric power basin" and cover an area of 14,500 square miles—"an area larger than Massachusetts, Connecticut and Rhode Island combined" that would extend across the border into Canada.[3]

Ernest Oberholtzer at his Mallard Island home in 1942. (Courtesy of Ernest C. Oberholtzer Foundation)

Of the hundreds of Rainy Lake residents who were concerned about the project, one man rose to take the lead in raising the objections that would defeat it. His name was Ernest Oberholtzer.

Oberholtzer was born and raised in Davenport, Iowa, and attended Harvard, where he studied landscape architecture under Frederick Law Olmsted and Sturgis Pray (the man who led young Benton MacKaye into the White Mountains to hike and construct trails). "Ober," as he was known to friends, displayed a natural talent for landscape design and worked with Olmsted's firm for one year before leaving the bustle of Brookline for the relative calm of Rainy Lake. In 1912, Oberholtzer made a two-thousand-mile round trip by canoe from Rainy Lake to Hudson Bay with an Ojibwe named Billy Magee, which established a lifelong friendship and instilled in Ober an appreciation for the wilderness that would inspire and inform his advocacy for it.

In September 1925, Ober took the first step in a new journey when he testified at the International Joint Commission on the Future of the Rainy Lake Watershed. The hosting commission had been established in

1909 by the United States and Great Britain (on behalf of Canada) to "evaluate, arbitrate and settle disputes arising along the shared boundary waters of the United States and Canada."[4]

Recalled Ober, "At the hearing [which lasted several days], I think there was only one person other than Mr. Backus who spoke in favor of his program. There were probably two hundred who didn't seem to like it."[5] But even though attendees felt good about their impact at the hearing, they were concerned about Backus's power. Within two years, it was clear who was best qualified to lead the pro-wilderness charge. Decades later he would write in a piece for his Harvard class's Fiftieth Anniversary Report, "It happens I was called upon in 1927 to take charge of this movement. This I agreed to do for only 6 months, but that was nearly 30 years ago. It was a night and day affair with no rest for the weary."[6]

By the late 1920s and early 1930s, Ernest Oberholtzer's growing impact in the wilderness movement was gaining national and international notice. It is not surprising that he would be asked to join another influential group before the decade was over. That he was able to make such an extraordinary impact from a modest compound in a quiet corner of the world is nothing short of remarkable.*

THE PROBLEM OF WILDERNESS
In February 1930, an article appeared in *Scientific Monthly* titled "The Problem of the Wilderness." Written by a twenty-nine-year-old forester, scientist, outdoorsman, and activist named Bob Marshall (not to be confused with the aforementioned Robert Marshall who worked for the NPS and USGS), the article thrust the idea of wilderness preservation into the public consciousness. In it, Marshall articulated the "physical, mental and ethestic [*sic*]" reasons why wilderness areas needed to be saved, advocated for conducting a federal study to identify such areas, and called for the organization of a group that would fight for the cause.[7]

In writing the article, Bob Marshall was making public a concern that he, Leopold, Oberholtzer, and a growing number of acquaintances—

---

*Ernest Oberholtzer is widely credited with impacting the preservation of more than 2.25 million acres of wilderness in northern Minnesota and southern Ontario, Canada. The Boundary Waters Canoe Area, Quetico-Superior area, and Voyageurs National Park can all trace their roots to "Ober."

foresters, outdoor enthusiasts, and conservationists among them—had about the proliferation of roads into the national landscape. Primitive areas were disappearing quickly, even within national forests and national parks. If something wasn't done soon to protect areas worth saving, it would be too late.

Marshall was a dynamic force in many regards and well suited to deliver a rallying cry. The son of a prominent, wealthy, and highly regarded civil rights lawyer (who had once been on the short list to be a

U.S. Supreme Court justice), Bob spent the summers of his youth at a family cottage in the Adirondacks. The forests and high peaks of the giant park were a playground for Bob and his brother George. It wasn't long before Bob became a local legend for his endurance hikes—scrambling over forty miles' worth of trails in a single day wasn't uncommon.

The preservation of the Adirondacks became an important cause for Bob's father, Louis Marshall, who rallied his neighbors when necessary to retain the spirit of the area. (It may be recalled that it was Louis Marshall who spoke out against Fernow's forestry school after the slash-pile fires inundated

Forester, scholar, author, and endurance hiker Bob Marshall was at the center of the emerging movement to establish wilderness areas. (U.S. Forest Service)

the area with smoke with the words, "This is scientific forestry?") Thus, his sons had been homeschooled in the subject of advocacy.

The same drive that propelled Bob Marshall over the highest peaks of New York established him in academic and professional life with remarkable speed. He earned a forestry degree from Syracuse in 1924, a master's in forestry from Harvard in 1925, spent over two years working for the Forest Service in Montana, then earned a PhD in plant physiology from Johns Hopkins in 1930. In between, he had spent fifteen months in Alaska, primarily in the Brooks Range, where he studied tree growth in the arctic climate.

His professional training, combined with time spent living in the wilderness, had led Marshall to believe that America was at an inflection point and that the greatest threat was the encroachment of roads. (The Forest Service alone had become a road building colossus, with an increase from a few thousand miles in 1916 to over 120,000 by 1935.[8]) Marshall called for immediate action. In "The Problem of Wilderness," he wrote,

Within the next few years, the fate of the wilderness must be decided. This is a problem to be settled by deliberate rationality and not by personal prejudice. Fundamentally, the question is one of balancing the total happiness, which will be obtainable if the few un-desecrated areas are perpetuated against that which will prevail if they are destroyed.[9]

Marshall realized that writing about the need to protect wilderness would only go so far, so he looked for ways to do something about it. In 1931 an opportunity came his way when he was asked to contribute a report on forest recreation for a Senate-sponsored analysis of the state of Forest Service lands. Marshall compiled a list of thirty-eight roadless areas in the United States, then set out to have the Forest Service designate the ones not already so declared as "primitive." In the words of Marshall biographer James M. Glover, the regional foresters who were asked to approve or deny Marshall's request "responded with the enthusiasm of the stone faces on Easter Island."[10]

Marshall's greatest contribution to the Copeland Report (published in March 1933) was a chapter titled "The Forest for Recreation," which presented the economic benefits of promoting recreation in national forests. Marshall identified seven types of recreation areas, most notably including "primeval areas"—defined as having "no permanent inhabitants, no roads, settlements, or power transportation. [Additionally] visitors would have to be self-sufficient for survival."[11] Though most of the report was not implemented, the work Marshall did in researching and preparing it would begin bearing fruit one year hence.

CHAPTER TWENTY-TWO

A New Society

IN 1932, AS THE DISAGREEMENTS REGARDING THE APPALACHIAN TRAIL were escalating between Benton MacKaye and Myron Avery, MacKaye received a letter from Harold Anderson. A prominent member of the Potomac Appalachian Trail Club, Anderson had recently toured the newly completed first thirty-four miles of Skyline Drive and was profoundly affected. He wrote,

> *The whole question of road vs. trail is very fundamental. We outdoor folk who love the primitive are accused of selfishness in trying to have preserved inviolate a narrow strip of the little we have left of the primitive area and preventing the enjoyment (?) by multitudes of the scenery of this area if roads were built thereon. It seems to me that it narrows down to the question of whether it is worthwhile to preserve the primitive.*[1]

As we have seen, MacKaye's immediate responses were to lobby the ATC to formally declare that the organization was against skyline drives and to impress on the public at large that a better option was to move scenic highways down onto the flanks of mountains and into valleys, with occasional visits to higher ground (as proposed in his "Flankline vs. Skyline" article). After neither one of those proposals gained traction, MacKaye set off in search of government employment. (The election of FDR presented new opportunities which MacKaye felt qualified to fill.)

In April 1933, MacKaye was hired by the U.S. commissioner of Indian affairs, John Collier, to help oversee forestry operations on reservations. Coincidentally, Collier had also hired Bob Marshall to head the agency's forestry division. MacKaye's employment would only last five months, but two friendships he established in that time would endure. On April 24, he met Bob Marshall for lunch. It was the first time they met, and it is hard to imagine that the two Harvard-educated foresters and wilderness advocates didn't find much to talk about. Yet MacKaye's stay in Washington and chance to establish a working relationship with Marshall was brief. MacKaye was dispatched to South Dakota for one week, then sent to Albuquerque, where he met Aldo Leopold, who had been sent there on a short-term assignment with the Forest Service. In the space of only a few weeks, some of the "spirited people who will fight for the freedom of the wilderness" had met and exchanged ideas. The once disparate voices were coming together.

KNOXVILLE BECKONS—TWICE

After Benton MacKaye was let go as part of an agency reshuffling, he fashioned an itinerary that included a stop in Knoxville, Tennessee, to make one more in-person acquaintance. Harvey Broome and MacKaye had been corresponding by mail for the past two years, largely about the fate of the AT. (In 1931, Broome had organized the annual ATC meeting in Knoxville and had urged MacKaye to attend. Although MacKaye did not attend, he asked Broome to read a message from him to the attendees, a plea to keep automobiles from trespassing on the trail.)[2]

An early member of the Smoky Mountains Hiking Club, Broome was so committed to hiking and wilderness issues that he gave up his job as a practicing attorney to become a law clerk so he could dedicate more time to the causes he loved. MacKaye and Broome's meeting quickly affirmed that the two would become great friends and advocates for the wilderness over the decades to come.

Although momentum was building, it would be nearly another year before the organizers of a sustainable wilderness movement would gather. That they did, and where they did is a fabled tale in conservation history.

In 1934, Harold Anderson was still rankled by the ATC's stance on Skyline Drive. He wrote a letter to Guy Frizzell, the president of the Smoky Mountains Hiking Club, suggesting the creation of a committee of four or five prominent hikers that could be empowered to "spike the Blue ridge skyline highway."[3] If the group failed, they could seek government support to move the AT over to the Alleghenies, where hikers could then enjoy a wilderness experience consistent with that originally proposed by MacKaye. Anderson's hope was that the core committee would evolve into a larger federation of hiking clubs. Anderson mailed his letter to Frizzell but also made a decision that would prove critical—he mailed a copy to MacKaye.

The same day MacKaye received the copy of Anderson's letter he received a telegram from Bob Marshall asking him to meet at the Andrew Johnson Hotel in Knoxville on August 11. MacKaye immediately decided to present Anderson's idea to Marshall.

When MacKaye and Broome, who had also been invited, met Marshall at the hotel, he quickly announced that he was in Knoxville on behalf of Secretary of the Interior Harold Ickes to scout possible routes for the "National Parkway" from Shenandoah to the Smokies. The irony was hardly lost on the group. In fact, MacKaye and Broome spent most of the evening devising an alternative route through the valleys below.* The next day, as they drove through the mountains following a stop at Newfound Gap, MacKaye, Marshall, and Broome discussed Anderson's proposal of forming a group to fight skyline drives. Marshall was enthusiastic, but he immediately advocated for a group with a broader reach, one that would work for the protection and preservation of the wilderness nationwide. The excited trio left the Smokies that day with a consensus to make it so.

One month later, Bob Marshall met Harold Anderson in Washington. The two agreed to organize the proposed wilderness

---

*Predictably, Marshall was critical of the parkway, leaving one to wonder why Ickes sent the advocate for roadless wilderness on a mission to scout the route. If Ickes was hoping Marshall would present reasons to kill the project, Marshall complied. He submitted the request shortly after he returned to Washington. But Ickes deferred the decision to Park Service director Arno Cammerer, who determined to proceed with the project.

group as quickly as possible. Anderson agreed to draft a statement of purpose. Marshall suggested inviting Aldo Leopold and Ernest Oberholtzer to join the organization.

On October 19, 1934, Benton MacKaye, Bob Marshall, Harvey Broome, Bernard Frank (a fellow forester who shared the group's views on roads and wilderness), and Frank's wife, Miriam, piled into Frank's car to make a field trip to a Civilian Conservation Corps camp north of Knoxville. The foresters were in town for the American Forestry Association's annual conference, where Marshall was slated to give that evening's keynote speech about his adventures in Alaska. The Frank party initially joined the caravan of conference attendees heading toward the CCC camp, but it didn't take long for their discussion about a new wilderness group to force a change of plans. The conversation became so animated that Bernard Frank pulled the car to the side of the road. The men ran up a roadside embankment and gathered around Marshall, who had pulled the organization's draft statement of principles from his pocket. Broome recalled the scene:

> One by one we took up matters of definition, philosophy, scope of work, name of organization, how we should launch the project, the names of persons that should sign the statement and those to whom it should be sent.[4]

By the time they scrambled back down the embankment, they were the founders of a new organization charged with "that extremely minor fraction of outdoor America which yet remains free from mechanical sights and sounds and smell." They named it the Wilderness Society.

An Invitation
In a letter dated October 19, 1934, Benton MacKaye sent an "Invitation to Help Organize a Group to Preserve the American Wilderness" (see full text in the appendix) to the six influential figures the fledgling organization hoped would join their cause.

The Wilderness Society Founders (*left to right*): Bernard Frank, Harvey Broome, Bob Marshall, and Benton MacKaye. Photo date unknown. (Courtesy of the Wilderness Society)

"The time has come, with the brutalizing pressure of a spreading metropolitan civilization, to recognize this wilderness environment as a serious human need rather than a luxury and plaything," the letter declared.[5]

John Collier (Marshall's former boss as the commissioner of Indian affairs) and John C. Merriam (paleontologist, conservationist, and associate of Robert Sterling Yard) declined. The four who accepted the invitation (Harold Anderson, Aldo Leopold, Ernest Oberholtzer, and Robert Sterling Yard) joined Benton MacKaye, Bob Marshall, Harvey Broome, and Bernhard Frank as the founders of the Wilderness Society.

The climb ahead would be long, steep, and ultimately successful, although some would not live long enough to reach the summit.

CHAPTER TWENTY-THREE

Drifting Along

FOR ITS FIRST ELEVEN YEARS, THE WILDERNESS SOCIETY ENDURED internal debates about its finances, membership, and, to a degree, its mission. To outsiders the organization was highly regarded and influential. In reality, the founders were often immersed in their own projects and found it difficult to serve the society in meaningful capacities.

The society's mission was never in doubt. The founders' dedication to preserving and protecting the country's wild lands was steadfast as ever. The question was who would guide them into their second decade and beyond.

The first significant, and nearly crippling, blow came only five years after the organization was founded when Bob Marshall was discovered deceased in the Pullman berth of a train he had boarded to travel from Washington to New York. He was just short of thirty-nine years old, and his death was almost incomprehensible to those who knew him as a friend and colleague. But his leadership role in the Wilderness Society left a daunting void. His connections were so vast and his ability to engage government agencies, conservation groups, and policy makers was unrivaled. There were also financial concerns. The society owed several debts that Marshall had promised to pay, but his record keeping had been haphazard and there was no money in the till to make things whole.

The society would soon learn that while Bob Marshall's record keeping may have left them wanting, his vision had not. Marshall's will had provided "for the creation of a charitable trust to preserve wilderness conditions in outdoor America and to increase the knowledge of citizens of the United States as to the importance of maintaining wilderness conditions in outdoor America for future generations."[1] His foresight and generosity enabled his beneficiary, the Wilderness Society, to navigate through one of its most precarious periods.

In May 1945, the society lost its second founding member when Robert Sterling Yard, its first and only president and the editor of its magazine, passed away at age eighty-four. Even though Yard's death had come after a period of steady decline, the organization didn't have a succession plan in place, which set forth a scramble to fill the void.

Of the six remaining founders, the two best suited to the job were least able to give up what they were doing. Ernest Oberholtzer was still living in the wilds of Minnesota on Mallard Island waging his effort to

Benton MacKaye, circa 1939. (Used with permission of the Shirley Historical Society)

preserve what would later become known as the Boundary Waters Canoe Area Wilderness. Living on his remote island, he was steering the successful campaign to preserve much of the Quetico-Superior area. Aldo Leopold was living in Baraboo, Wisconsin, where he and his family had restored a shack and were experimenting with prairie restoration, and where Leopold would find inspiration for developing his land ethic and writing his influential book of essays, *A Sand County Almanac*. Two of the other founding members were also too busy to take on the role of president. Bernard Frank was active in four other conservation associations. Harvey Broome was channeling most of his energy into protecting the Great Smoky Mountains near his Tennessee home. Thus in 1945, sixty-six-year-old Benton MacKaye became the second president of the Wilderness Society, a job he would hold for five years.

All changes of organizational leadership expose strengths and weaknesses. In this case, whereas Yard was an inspiring communicator who steered the society's newsletter *The Living Wilderness* to national prominence and ensured that the reasons for protecting wilderness were clearly articulated for its readers, MacKaye faced an uphill battle. While unquestionably brilliant, his ideas swirled in a realm that challenged direct, meaningful connections. (He had once acknowledged as much to his regional planning colleague, Lewis Mumford, asking him, "Why should I ever write myself, when you can portray my ideas so much better?")[2] With *The Living Wilderness* magazine so critical to the society's visibility and growth, it needed to hire a talented writer to take over the job. They didn't need to cast about for long.

Howard Zahniser had earned a reputation around Washington, DC, as a hardworking researcher, editor, and writer. He'd been employed by several federal agencies for fifteen years, including the Department of Commerce, the U.S. Fish and Wildlife Service, and the USDA. When the Wilderness Society job opened up, there was a wee bit of skepticism on both sides. Some of the Wilderness Society founders believed that Zahniser "looked more like a librarian than a wilderness guy" and wondered if he was cut out for the job. Zahniser's concern was with the salary. He'd sacrifice at least 50 percent of his government salary to join the nonprofit, a decision his spouse, Alice, supported.[3]

Governing council member Harvey Broome later recalled his reaction to meeting "Zahnie" and his failure to then realize that both sides were making a gamble.

> *I had a great respect for Bob Yard and wondered whether this "youngster" could fill his shoes. It never occurred to me that day that his very coming to the young Society was an act of extraordinary faith and dedication on his part; for, with a very young family, he had given up secure employment to take over a still uncertain job.*[4]

STEEPED IN NATURE
Howard Zahniser was born in Franklin, Pennsylvania, in 1906. His family moved frequently during his early childhood because of his father's

Howard Zahniser worked tirelessly to make *The Living Wilderness* magazine a leading voice for conservation-minded leaders and readers while simultaneously nurturing the Wilderness Bill toward passage. (U.S. Fish and Wildlife Service)

occupation as a Free Methodist minister. When Howard was twelve, the family settled in the Allegheny River town of Tionesta, Pennsylvania, which instilled a wonder for nature in the boy, especially after he was fitted with spectacles and could fully appreciate the beauty around him. Like Benton MacKaye, young Zahniser enjoyed exploring the woods and hills near his home. He was also influenced by his teachers, one of whom started a chapter of Junior Audubon, which led to a lifelong fascination with birds.[5]

The Tionesta area held such importance to Zahniser that he and his wife, Alice, honeymooned by paddling a canoe down the Allegheny from Ocean, New York, to Howard's hometown.

In addition to being outdoors, Zahniser was influenced by the philosophers and nature writers that preceded him. He owned thousands of books; seldom traveled without a copy of *Walden*, the book of Job, *Palgrave's Golden Treasury of English Verse*, or Dante's *Inferno* along for inspiration; and visited bookstores wherever he traveled. His son Edward recalled that when the bookshelves at home were filled, his father would store additional books in the trunk of the family car.[6]

As his career gained traction and the family grew to include four children, Zahniser would spend more time writing about nature than being in it. But as time would show, he was more of a wilderness man than any of the Wilderness Society's surviving founders could have imagined.

IMMEDIATE IMPACT

Howard Zahniser was a gifted writer and editor. That alone would have ensured that *The Living Wilderness* held its status as the preeminent conservation publication. But there was more. Realizing that the magazine could serve a greater role in building a wilderness movement, he created a "News Notes" section that cited the goings-on within like-minded organizations (and in turn initiated dialogue among them). It was an act of genius that environmental historian T. H. Watkins declared was "Zahniser's greatest contribution to environmental journalism."[7] The feeling was echoed by his son Edward, who noted that "the many bridges to other groups first built through the magazine's news section eventually helped fashion the first national conservation coalition."[8]

To make sure the issues of *The Living Wilderness* were as timely as possible, Zahniser would drive from Hyattsville, Maryland, to Baltimore with galley prints and son Edward in tow, then write the magazine's editorial and squeeze in bulletins and newsworthy items right up until the magazine went to press.[9]

THE BLACK RIVER WARS

Only a few months into his job as executive secretary and editor at the Wilderness Society, Howard Zahniser attended the North American Wildlife Conservation Conference in New York. While there, he met Paul Schaefer and John Apperson, who made a presentation about proposed dams on the Moose River within New York's Adirondack State Park. Schaefer and Apperson showed a movie to the audience detailing how the proposed project in the western Adirondacks would flood a significant amount of lowland that was important winter deer yarding habitat. After the film, Zahniser approached the podium and "told Schaefer that The Wilderness Society would help defend the western Adirondacks against dams."[10] Joining the cause, which would become known as the Black River Wars, would be Zahniser's first foray into active wilderness preservation, and what he learned from the campaign accelerated his trajectory as a wilderness advocate.

Schaefer, Apperson, and Zahniser made an effective team. Schaefer possessed great grassroots organizing skills, Apperson provided the hellfire (his motto for engaging constituents was "We will wake them up!"), and Zahniser had the connections and publicity experience to get the word out. Schaefer and Zahniser traveled all over the western Adirondacks "testifying at public hearings, meeting with news people, and identifying and cultivating local advocates of wildlands" to drum up opposition to the dams.[11] Despite the fact that the project had been officially approved by the state of New York, Schafer, Apperson, and Zahniser were able to line up more than one thousand local and national organizations to defeat the project.[12]

Turning back the dam project provided several important lessons for Zahniser and affirmed the work he had already been doing to connect various organizations interested in protecting the wildness of federal and state lands. Schaefer and Apperson had shown him how to build a grassroots campaign firsthand and how to "stump for the wilderness" by engaging audiences and inspiring action. To be successful in any such campaign, Apperson advised, you must "stand on the land you want to save. Take pictures so the public sees what is at stake."[13]

What Howard Zahniser learned in the Adirondacks would pay national dividends four years hence.

CHAPTER TWENTY-FOUR

Man with a Mission

THE SUCCESS IN THE ADIRONDACKS HAD BEEN BOTH SATISFYING AND exhausting for Howard Zahniser. But he and the other leaders of the Wilderness Society had already charted a course that they hoped would not require defending the sanctity of wild areas as they were individually threatened.

The leadership of the Wilderness Society had identified the immediate threats. The first was dams, which codirector of the organization Olaus Murie felt were the "greatest threat to primeval America."[1]

The second threat was timber harvesting. Driven largely by new home construction, "postwar national forest managers were active in opening vast forest areas to timber management."[2] The timber industry that had formerly preferred to keep timber harvesting in national forests low to help keep the prices of timber harvested from their own and other privately held wood lots high "now sought cheap national forest timber to supplement or replace heavily cutover private forest lands."[3]

One of Zahniser's suggestions to the Wilderness Society elders was to hold their annual board meetings in proximity to the areas they were working to protect. In 1947, the meeting was held at Ernest Oberholtzer's Mallard Island compound on Rainy Lake in northernmost Minnesota. Since Zahniser's appointment as executive secretary two years before, Benton MacKaye had been formulating a plan to move the organization to launch a national legislative initiative to establish and protect wilderness areas. Like Zahniser, MacKaye was weary of playing defense. At the 1947 Mallard Island meeting, the governing council of the Wilderness Society adopted MacKaye's suggestion "to focus the society's work on securing a nationwide system of wilderness areas more securely protected by statutory law."[4] MacKaye astutely advised that this decision would align the organization with positive action, standing for the wilderness versus being against projects or progress.

In a letter to Wilderness Society members following the 1947 annual meeting, MacKaye debuted the concept of a wilderness bill.

The Wilderness Society Council, at the 1947 annual meeting held last June in the Quetico-Superior country, in the heart of North America, took occasion to launch from this pivotal area a campaign for renewed effort to extend throughout the continent a system of wilderness areas. The spots of wilderness that would result should be every type of country from Alaskan tundra to Canadian conifer to Florida everglade.[5]

There was no doubt who in the Wilderness Society would be leading the effort to establish federal wilderness legislation, and Zahniser took it on with admirable zeal. As he saw it, he needed to make compelling cases for why wilderness areas were needed (what made them different from other public lands) and for clearly defining what wilderness areas were (and were not) and how they could be managed. Concurrently, he would need to build alliances and earn legislative support—"to stand on the land" and articulate what was at stake. It was an enormous task, one that required every bit of Howard Zahniser's skills and energy.

It would also take the help of someone who could help create a game plan for guiding a bill through Congress. Ernest Griffith, the director of the Legislative Reference Service (and a member of the Wilderness Society's governing council), advised Zahniser that the first step in getting wilderness legislation passed was to launch an inventory of wilderness areas. He urged "Zahnie" to convince a legislator to formally "request from the Legislative Reference Bureau an inventory of wilderness and wild areas in the United States."[6] (That legislator turned out to be U.S. House of Representatives member John P. Saylor of Pennsylvania.)

As a prerequisite to preparing the report (likely with Griffith's guidance), the bureau sent a questionnaire "seeking opinions from many quarters"[7] regarding whether they believed legislation to establish wilderness areas was needed and, if so, how they would recommend establishing and managing such lands.

Released in 1949, *The Preservation of Wilderness Areas, an Analysis of Opinion on the Problem* provided a comprehensive list of wild lands and recommendations for the successful establishment and administration of a potential wilderness act. These were as follows:

- A simple, clear definition [of wilderness] that is not too restrictive
- National legislation given equal status with national parks policy
- Clearly defined permissible and prohibited uses for wilderness areas

The creator of the report, an economist named C. Frank Keyser, concluded that

> *nearly all [parties surveyed] agree that the permanence of the wilderness nature of these areas must be provided for in any statement of national policy, most of them believing it should be to the same degree as that assuring the permanence of national parks.*[8]

The impressive report was the first piece of Wilderness Act material that Zahniser shopped around Congress to begin building consensus for legislation. Importantly, the report established that there was broad interest in preserving wilderness areas. But it also gave Howard Zahniser a blueprint for drafting the legislation itself.

Wilderness Society leaders knew that there were two important components of building congressional support—making personal connections and appeals to legislators and gaining broad-based support from their constituents. To begin doing the latter, Benton MacKaye suggested holding a series of biennial wilderness conferences to keep the issue in the public eye. (MacKaye's suggestion was likely spurred by the conferences that had helped gain substantial and critical early support for the Appalachian Trail.) MacKaye further suggested that the Sierra Club host the event, an invitation the organization's *Bulletin* editor David Brower and his colleagues enthusiastically accepted.

The first biennial wilderness conference, held in San Francisco on April 7 and 8, 1949, brought together a who's who of conservationists (Brower, Howard Zahniser, Roderick Nash, Ian McTaggart-Cowan, Frank Fraser Darling, Starker Leopold, and Luna Leopold), politicians (Senator Henry "Scoop" Jackson, Governor Edmund G. "Pat" Brown, congressman and future interior secretary Stewart Udall, and Congressman John Saylor), as well as representatives of the Forest Service, the National Park Service, and the Bureau of Land Management. Also represented were fishing guides, loggers, backcountry guides, and others with economic interests in public lands.

The two-day event was packed with speeches, films, slide shows, presentations of papers, and most important, "discussions about the meaning of wilderness to science, wildlands to our civilization, and other wilderness-related matters, all aimed, at least informally, toward building the rationale and support for an eventual national law to protect wilderness permanently."[9]

Always seeking to broaden support for wilderness protection, Brower compiled the speeches and presentations from the conference, complemented them with his own editorial, and had them published under the Sierra Club imprint. But the conference had also served a more immediate need. The consensus and the alliances built over those few days would be tested and strengthened in a battle to preserve public lands.

THE ECHO PARK DAM PROJECT

In 1949 the U.S. Bureau of Reclamation proposed building two dams within Dinosaur National Monument as part of their upper Colorado River storage project. The creation of Echo Park Dam and the smaller Split Mountain dam would flood two canyons, destroy dinosaur fossil mounds, and redefine the topography of the entire area. Steamboat Rock, one of the park's iconic features named by intrepid explorer John Wesley Powell on his way through the region, would retain only one-third of its height above river level after its base was consumed by rising water.

The project proceeded for three years with little public outcry. That began to change in 1952 when a man named Harold Bradley traveled down the Yampa River through the proposed dam site with two of his sons and their families. After their weeklong trip, they emerged with a few reels of home movies and a newfound dedication to preventing the Echo Park Dam from being built. The Bradley family had known the legendary wilderness disciple John Muir and were familiar with his unsuccessful battle to prevent the Hetch Hetchy dam's construction.

Bradley feared that if the Echo Park Dam was built, nothing would prevent other dams from being constructed in other national parks and monuments, acts that undermined the intent of their very being. So Bradley packed up his film projector and began showing his movie footage to audiences throughout the western states. Bradley's lecture was all the new executive director of the Sierra Club, David Brower, needed to see to swing into action.

Brower was already a passionate defender of the wilderness and had run into the problem of a once declared "primitive area" being rescinded by a federal agency in his recent past. In 1931, the Forest Service established the nearly thirty-two-thousand-acre San Gorgonio Mountain Primitive Area. A decade later, responding to developers of a proposed ski resort, they redrew the boundary of the protected area to accommodate "lodges, a ski resort, and rope tows up the north slopes of Jepson Peak and San Gorgonio."[10] After a contentious public meeting in 1941, the plan to develop the primitive area was tabled through the end of the war. But in December 1946, the issue resurfaced when the regional forester announced the resubmission of the resort plan. A ninety-day notice and public hearing were all that stood in the way of the groundbreaking.

Brower and his colleagues were incensed. What use was a wilderness designation if it could be rescinded any time with the stroke of a pen? Editor Brower went into action. In the January 1947 issue of the *Sierra Club Bulletin*, he wrote,

> *The wilderness concept is on trial, is up for sacrifice under the guise of compromise. . . . Where wilderness is concerned, there can be no compromise. Wilderness, like life itself, is absolute. A man cannot literally be half dead or half alive. He is dead or he is alive. A developed area cannot be wild.*[11]

Brower's passionate plea to preserve the San Gorgonio Primitive Area helped win the day. In June 1947, Forest Service chief Lyle F. Watts announced the agency's determination that "the San Gorgonio Primitive Area [had] higher public value as a wilderness and a watershed than as a downhill ski area."[12]

Shortly after the announcement that the wilderness status of the area had been retained, Howard Zahniser wrote a piece for *Land Policy Review* declaring that,

for the first time, the strength of the widespread demand for safeguarding the Nation's primitive areas was demonstrated. For the first time the real use of such an area was revealed in detail. For the first time, in the face of a clear-cut issue, the national determination to preserve what primeval areas are still so available, even in the face of otherwise highly worthy demands, was made manifest. No one—not even the most earnest of wilderness preservers—had realized how great this demand, this use, this determination, had become.[13]

Zahniser concluded his piece by urging those who care about wilderness to use the unprecedented victory as an example of what can be achieved. Citing Bob Marshall's landmark essay of 1930, "The Problem of the Wilderness," he wrote, "For some time to come, anyone who prizes these areas but who is tempted to be discouraged in the face of the 'tyrannical ambition of civilization to conquer every niche on the whole earth' can well remember the San Gorgonio."[14]

As it turned out, the celebration for saving San Gorgonio would be short lived, as the resistance to the Echo Park Dam would require a brilliantly executed campaign and every bit of David Brower's and Howard Zahniser's collective energies.

Opposition to the dam project gained unprecedented speed as Brower created what his son Kenneth described as the "prototypic conservation campaign as we know it today."[15] Brower organized several Sierra Club–sponsored trips down the Yampa River so that hundreds of people would experience firsthand the grandeur of a place on the verge of being lost forever. He convinced publisher Alfred A. Knopf to commission a book of photographs and essays to be edited by the dean of western writers, Wallace Stegner, then brilliantly sent a copy to every member of Congress.[16]

The Sierra Club commissioned a documentary film by Charles Eggert highlighting the beauty and historical value of Dinosaur National Monument. Written by Brower, the film also addressed the issue of progress, explicitly stating that the conservationists were not against it—an important distinction that would be revisited in campaigns to come. As the film ended, Brower narrated,

> We all know that progress must move forward. Sometimes it will march upright with sound development. Sometimes it will stumble and make a slum. Certainly, we can ask progress to walk around and not through our garden, America's parklands. . . . Similar dam sites, above and below Dinosaur, can provide Utah with more water storage and more kilowatts than can be obtained by spoiling Dinosaur National Monument with dams and reservoirs. We can have both if we approach the problem with open minds. Water and power and a unique unspoiled asset for Utah and all of the rest of the country, too. All of us who must pay the piper cannot let a few people call the tune—a dirge for Dinosaur.[17]

Brower also mounted PR and lobbying campaigns aimed at decision makers in Washington, DC. David Brower's chief ally in Washington was Howard Zahniser, who built a consortium of supporters that included former First Lady Eleanor Roosevelt and seventeen organizations that voiced their opposition to the dam. As the controversy peaked, Zahniser also used Brower and Eggert's film to advantage. "[He] rolled a film projector on a dolly through congressional office buildings, pigeonholing anyone he came across and showing the film. Several ended up in tears."[18]

In 1954, David Brower summed up the case for protecting national parks monuments as intended. "The axiom for protecting the Park System," he wrote, "is to consider that it is dedicated country, hallowed ground to leave as beautiful as we have found it, and not country in which man should be so impressed with himself that he tries to improve God's handiwork."[19]

When the Colorado River Storage Project Act became law on April 11, 1956, it stated that "no dam or reservoir constructed under the authorization of the Act shall be within any national park or monument."

While the construction of the Echo Park and Split Mountain dams was removed from consideration, the victory came with a cost. The U.S. Bureau of Land Reclamation insisted that the environmental groups that opposed the dams would not oppose the construction of the Glen Canyon Dam and the Flaming Gorge Dam as part of the agreement.

(While it initially seemed like a reasonable request, Brower would look back at the terms of the agreement with deep regret. He had not visited Glen Canyon until after the Colorado River Storage Project Act was signed. Once he saw the beauty of the canyon, he was stunned. For the rest of his life, he wondered if he could have saved Glen Canyon if he had done more, and he chastised himself for not visiting the site before agreeing to the terms of the act. Biographer Tom Turner wrote that "it was the single most wrenching experience of his life—a lesson he vowed to learn and never repeat.")[20]

Nonetheless, Brower and Zahniser's powerful partnership and coordinated efforts made history. Building on the foundation laid by John Muir and Robert Underwood Johnson more than a generation before, their campaign to save Dinosaur National Monument set a new standard for raising national awareness and inspiring action to protect existing public lands. Indeed, author Jon Cosco, in researching the events surrounding the campaign, concluded that, "if with the benefit of hindsight, we can claim that the modern environmental movement had some clearly recognizable beginning, we might start to look for it in a scenic canyon called Echo Park."[21]

CHAPTER TWENTY-FIVE

A Wilderness Forever

We are not fighting progress. We are making it. We are not dealing with
the vanishing wilderness. We are working for a wilderness forever.
—HOWARD ZAHNISER

IT WOULD HAVE BEEN UNDERSTANDABLE IF HOWARD ZAHNISER SAW
the Echo Park Dam campaign as yet another example of the kinds of
"overlapping emergencies, threats and defense campaigns" he felt were
diverting conservationists away from the important work of securing
national wilderness land legislation. But it had the opposite effect. In fact,
the coalition of organizations, citizens, opinion writers, and government
officials and agencies that he and David Brower assembled gave him
hope that a wilderness act was within reach.

Historian Doug Scott wrote that the Echo Park campaign "became
by far the most significant conservation campaign of the twentieth
century. Later battles—and notably the campaign for the Wilderness
Act—were won with strategic and tactical tools that Zahniser, the Sierra
Club's David Brower, and their colleagues forged and protected in the
Echo Park campaign."[1]

Zahniser realized that capitalizing on the momentum built by the
campaign would take a larger coalition still. To earn it, he needed to
define and continually refine the terms of the mission, and he needed to
win the support of legislators and government agencies, most notably the

Park Service and Forest Service, who, on the face of things, stood to lose influence and control.

An important aspect of gaining broad-based support was emphasizing that the creation of wilderness areas was not a crusade against progress. Rather, Zahniser saw the establishment and protection of wilderness areas as a human necessity—vital to our well-being and our very existence.

In a 1955 speech that was later reprinted in *The Living Wilderness,* Zahniser made his case that we need

> *areas of wild nature in which we sense ourselves to be, what I in fact believe we are, dependent members of an interdependent community of living creatures that together derive their existence from the sun. By very definition this wilderness is a need. The idea of wilderness as an area without man's influence is man's own concept. Its values are human values. Its preservation is a purpose that arises out of man's own sense of his fundamental needs.* [2]

THE WILDERNESS BILL

In 1956, Howard Zahniser wrote the first draft of what would become the Wilderness Bill. It called for the creation of a national wilderness system that would retain their wilderness character and be free from roads and motorized vehicles. To engage members of Congress, federal agencies, and the American public, Zahniser built consensus in the tradition of his upbringing, slowly and purposefully. "His father was a minister and made a lot of pastoral calls," said son Edward. "I think a lot of my father's approach toward congressional visits was to treat it the same way. You never took no for an answer. You always came back to see if they were ready for the kingdom." [3]

Listening to the concerns of representatives and senators, responding to them frequently, and operating with no timetable other than what was required to win support was an approach few legislators had ever known. He sought "to see the virtues in opponents' arguments,

Harvey Broome and Howard Zahniser working on the Wilderness Bill at the Broome homestead in Tennessee. (National Park Service)

striving to find a way, if he could, to meet their objections." Moreover, "he did not see opponents as enemies; he genuinely coveted coming to some understanding whereby their interests and his for wilderness preservation could be reconciled."[4]

Fellow Wilderness Society Executive Council member Harvey Broome wrote down his impressions of Zahniser after one of the latter's visits to the Broome home early in the days of the Wilderness Bill campaign:

> *Zahnie has a very great talent. He is a genius at resolving differences and at getting along with people. He can do a prodigious amount of work. He has a self-confidence that is not overbearing. He has great vision, great conviction, and a great breadth of interest. Others lean on him—sense his strength. He can differ without getting personal. He can recognize unworthy motivations or shallowness in others*

without becoming disdainful. He has an imperturbable momentum which carries him through a conflict without a mark. He is a great and essentially a humble man.[5]

In addition to his demeanor, Zahniser employed an ingenious piece of gear specially constructed for his wanderings through the halls of Congress in quest of support for the Wilderness Bill. He took his favorite overcoat to a local tailor and had him sew so many pockets inside it that the coat functioned as a filing cabinet. Inside, Zahnie carried different versions of talking points regarding the Wilderness Bill, which he could present at a moment's notice to legislators he met on his way to and from meetings. He also carried a favorite paperback or two in case he had time to read between appointments. Son Edward recalled that lifting the coat to hang it on a hook or over the back of a chair was akin to lifting weights and that the family always got a good laugh out of the nightly ritual.[6]

The greatest obstacle Zahniser and his cohorts, both inside and outside the Wilderness Society, faced was confronting misconceptions about both the intention of the Wilderness Bill and the effect it would have. Not surprisingly, the greatest objections were voiced by the lumber, mining, and ranching communities. But the Forest Service and National Park Service also cried foul. Zahniser was "particularly disheartened by the position of the National Park Service, which saw the bill as a critique of its own mission and strongly opposed it."[7]

To clarify the purpose of the bill, dispel misconceptions, and mitigate concerns, would require a long, steady march—the kind that suited Zahnie more than most, or perhaps anyone else. And to do it, he went straight to the audiences whose trust he needed to win. The following remarks from a speech he gave before the Society of American Foresters on March 14, 1957, exemplified Zahniser's approach.

It has long been my opinion . . . that wilderness preservation policies in this country will not be firmly established and secure until those who might wish to make conflicting use of our wilderness areas have joined in developing such policies and, having done so, are satisfied to accept them.

That includes foresters. It most emphatically includes foresters. I can think of no group of people who can be so personally interested in the preservation of primeval forests as are foresters. I can think of no man so deeply concerned as a forester is with having examples of the primeval still living for his children, and theirs, and theirs, on and on, to see and know. Our modern, our current, movement for wilderness preservation was led by foresters, and to a great extent the success of our wilderness preservation efforts now will be determined by foresters.[8]

As the months, revisions, and meetings went on, Zahniser continued to slowly build support for the Wilderness Bill by "widening the consensus to the point where it comprises the majority."[9] In practical terms, that required nineteen congressional hearings, sixty plus rewrites of the legislation, scores of meetings and appearances with audiences across the country, writing articles for newspapers, and finding support wherever he could. Through it all, he consistently emphasized that "we are not advocating a program for The Wilderness Society . . . we are advocating a program for the people of the United States of America."[10]

The message that the wilderness was not to be preserved for the few, but that it was part of every human's experience, was central to Zahniser's message. In a 1961 speech to the Sierra Club, he said,

Out of the wilderness has come the substance of our culture, and with a living wilderness—it is our faith—we shall also have a vibrant, vital culture, an enduring civilization of healthful, happy people who . . . perpetually renew themselves in contact with the earth. We not only value the wilderness because of its own superlative values but because our experience in the wilderness meets fundamental human needs. These needs are not only recreational and spiritual, but also educational and scientific, not only personal but cultural. They are profound. For wilderness is essential to us, as human beings, for a true understanding of ourselves, our culture, our own natures, our place in all nature.[11]

"Widening the circle" enough to gain passage of the Wilderness Bill was one of the greatest achievements in America's conservation history. But Zahnie would not live long enough to see it signed into law.

Howard Zahniser went to sleep on May 4, 1964, with the knowledge and contentment that the Wilderness Bill was headed for approval. Sometime in the morning hours of May 5, just four days after testifying at the last of the congressional hearings on the Wilderness Bill, his heart gave out. He was fifty-eight years old.

Longtime colleague and executive director of the Sierra Club, David Brower, who had worked with Zahnie as far back as the Echo Dam project, noted the passing of his friend by saying,

Passage of the wilderness bill can be hailed as the most significant conservation development in this decade and perhaps the most significant since the National Park Act of 1916. The values that are in the Wilderness Act are in large part a tribute to Howard Zahniser's fidelity, to his patient, devoted years. He was able to make wilderness everybody's business. He engaged the most effective of allies and the honor roll is long. . . . But what made the difference was one man's conscience, his tireless search for a way to put national wilderness policy into law, his talking and writing and persuading, his living so this act might be born. The hardest times were those when good friends tired because the battle was so long. Urging those friends back into action was the most anxious part of Howard Zahniser's work. It succeeded but took his last energy.[12]

The *New York Times* observed that "there is a special poignancy in the death of a man on the apparent eve of his attaining the goal for which he had long and devotedly labored."[13]

In July 1964, the full House passed the wilderness bill by a vote of 374 to 1. On September 3, 1964, President Lyndon Johnson signed the

President Lyndon Johnson signs the Wilderness Act into law on September 3, 1964.
(National Park Service)

National Wilderness Act into law with Howard Zahniser's widow, Alice,
Harvey Broome, and several more friends and colleagues looking on.

Howard Zahniser had given it his all to draft a bill that would earn
majority support. Now it was up to the American people and their legislators to identify and protect the living wilderness forever.

Chapter Twenty-Six

Legacy

In 1864, when Frederick Law Olmsted stood in Yosemite Valley, there were no national parks. Yet he and a growing number of forward thinkers had already come to the realization that saving such places was critical to the nation's identity and prosperity.

But creating a vision and bringing it to life are rarely achieved by one person, even one as dynamic as Olmsted himself. Thus, the story of America's conservation history—the creation of our national forests, national parks, and wilderness areas—is the story of triumph, failure, ego, humility, heroes (both sung and unsung), and, most of all, perseverance.

It is an enduring example of the importance of mentorship, the evolution of ideas implemented from one generation to the next, and an inspiration for those of us committed to protecting the natural world to carry on. Establishing public lands is difficult. Maintaining them for the benefit of everyone—ourselves, our children, their children, and so on—is our task.

One month before his death, with the Wilderness Bill passage almost assured, Howard Zahniser made a speech in Portland, Oregon, that mirrored thoughts often expressed by his good friend David Brower—that passing legislation was an important step, but the true work would begin after the signing ceremony and require ongoing diligence.

We have fought most of the battle on the national front. A good many wars are won on the battlegrounds and lost at the peace treaty. I hope

The Gifford Pinchot National Forest includes the former blast zone of Mount St. Helens, where the forest is staging a comeback. (Author photo)

that won't be the case now. But it seems to me that as we see adopted the national policy of wilderness preservation by Congress that will be sustained by the present consensus, it's up to us to start now, as citizens, to influence our fellow citizens in the most effective way to get the maximum amount of wilderness preserved in the most enduring fashion that we possibly can.[1]

THE STATUS OF PUBLIC LANDS TODAY

True to both David Brower's and Howard Zahniser's predictions, the efforts to establish and retain the status of public lands in the half century since the passage of the Wilderness Act have been challenging. Efforts to rescind the establishment of national monuments or redraw their boundaries to favor extractive industries have threatened the existence of public lands from Maine to Alaska. But there are also hopeful signs.

167

"Conservation vs. Preservation"

If one word could encapsulate the history of the creation of America's public lands, "contentious" would be it. One consistent source of friction, even among those dedicated to our public spaces, has been how they should be managed (the creation of Adirondack Park and the battle over Hetch Hetchy are the best examples of that ongoing debate).

For over 150 years, most people concerned with public lands readily identified as either conservationists (aligned with Pinchot's view that public lands should be managed resources) or preservationists (aligned with Muir's view that public lands should be left alone).

But there are signs of the two camps coming together over two common threats. The advent of climate change and the stunning collapse of biodiversity (and the attendant increase in species extinction) are reframing the conversation.

On the conservation side, foresters are adopting the stance that trees can be harvested less frequently. Simply allowing the largest trees to stand for a few more years allows them to absorb and store more carbon. Adopting a "thinning and harvesting" approach still allows the forest to be productive and profitable while also improving wildlife habitat.[2]

On the preservation side, advocates for protected land are launching new initiatives to "rewild" tracts of land that have been deforested or otherwise impacted, then preserved forever as wilderness. It is an idea that harkens to Aldo Leopold and his family's efforts to restore a piece of practically worthless Wisconsin farmland by planting tens of thousands of trees and rare prairie grasses.

One significant rewilding project is taking place in the northeastern United States. Spearheaded by the Northeast Wilderness Trust, the effort has already established nearly fifty thousand acres as "the old growth forests of tomorrow" in New England and New York. In some cases, the land has been logged and will be restored on nature's terms following nature's timetable. These wild places, "where nature calls the shots," will safeguard biodiversity, absorb and store carbon as a means of combating climate change, and welcome those "who come to experience solitude, wildlife, and beauty, with reverence and care for the land's integrity."[3]

THE BATON IS OURS TO CARRY NOW

The story of the creation of America's many kinds of public lands has been one of generational baton passes. Frederick Law Olmsted hired Gifford Pinchot, who, in turn, hired the foresters who became the founders of the Wilderness Society. The generations that followed were charged with protecting and caring for the public lands those pioneers had the foresight to establish. We still have an opportunity to make good on our obligation.

Will we?

Appendix

1: The Article That Launched the Appalachian Trail

The article below, published in the *Journal of the American Institute of Architects* in October 1921, launched the concept of the Appalachian Trail into the public consciousness.

An Appalachian Trail: A Project in Regional Planning
By Benton MacKaye

Something has been going on in this country during the past few strenuous years which, in the din of war and general upheaval, has been somewhat lost from the public mind. It is the slow quiet development of a special type of community—the recreation camp. It is something neither urban nor rural. It escapes the hecticness of the one, the loneliness of the other. And it escapes also the common curse of both—the high powered tension of the economic scramble. All communities face an "economic" problem, but in different ways. The camp faces it through cooperation and mutual helpfulness, the others through competition and mutual fleecing.

We civilized ones also, whether urban or rural, are potentially as helpless as canaries in a cage. The ability to cope with nature directly—unshielded by the weakening wall of civilization—is one of the admitted needs of modern times. It is the goal of the "scouting" movement. Not that we want to return to the plights of our Paleolithic ancestors. We want the strength of progress without its puniness. We want its conveniences without its fopperies. The ability to sleep and cook in the open is a good step forward. But "scouting" should not stop there. This is but a faint step from our canary bird existence. It should strike much deeper than this.

We should seek the ability not only to cook food but to raise food with less aid—and less hindrance—from the complexities of commerce. And this is becoming daily of increasing practical importance. Scouting, then, has its vital connection with the problem of living.

A New Approach to the Problem of Living

The problem of living is at bottom an economic one. And this alone is bad enough, even in a period of so-called "normalcy." But living has been considerably complicated of late in various ways—by war, by questions of personal liberty, and by "menaces" of one kind or another. There have been created bitter antagonisms. We are undergoing also the bad combination of high prices and unemployment. This situation is world wide—the result of a world-wide war.

It is no purpose of this little article to indulge in coping with any of these big questions. The nearest we come to such effrontery is to suggest more comfortable seats and more fresh air for those who have to consider them. A great professor once said that "optimism is oxygen." Are we getting all the "oxygen" we might for the big tasks before us?

"Let us wait," we are told, "til we solve this cussed labor problem. Then we'll have the leisure to do great things."

But suppose that while we wait the chance for doing them is passed?

It goes without saying we should work upon the labor problem. Not just the matter of "capital and labor" but the *real* labor problem—how to reduce the day's drudgery. The toil and chore of life should, as labor saving devices increase, form a diminishing proportion of the average day and year. Leisure and higher pursuits will thereby come to form an increasing proportion of our lives.

But will leisure mean something "higher"? Here is a question indeed. The coming of leisure in itself will create its own problem. As the problem of labor "solves," that of leisure arises. There seems to be no escape from problems. We have neglected to improve the leisure which should be ours as a result of replacing stone and bronze with iron and steam. Very likely we have been cheated out of the bulk of this leisure. The efficiency of modern industry has been placed at 25 per cent of its reasonable possibilities. This may be too low or too high. But the leisure that we do succeed in getting—is this developed to an efficiency much higher?

The customary approach to the problem of living relates to work rather than play. Can we increase the efficiency of our *working* time? Can we solve the problem of labor? If so we can widen the opportunities of our leisure. The new approach reverses this mental process. Can we increase the efficiency of our *spare* time? Can we develop opportunities for leisure as an aid in solving the problem of labor?

An Undeveloped Power—Our Spare Time

How much spare time have we, and how much power does it represent?

The great body of working people—the industrial workers, the farmers, and the housewives—have no allotted spare time or "vacations." The business clerk usually gets two weeks' leave, with pay, each year. The U.S. Government clerk gets thirty days. The business man is likely to give himself two weeks or a month. Farmers can get off for a week or more at a time by doubling up on one another's chores. Housewives might do likewise.

As to the industrial worker—in mine or factory—his average "vacation" is all too long. For it is "leave of absence *without* pay." According to recent official figures the average industrial worker in the United States, during normal times, is employed in industry about four fifths of the time—say 42 weeks in the year. The other ten weeks he is employed in seeking employment.

The proportionate time for true leisure of the average adult American appears, then, to be meagre indeed. But a goodly portion have (or take) about two weeks in the year. The industrial worker during the estimated ten weeks between jobs must of course go on eating and living. His savings may enable him to do this without undue worry. He could, if he felt he could spare the time from job hunting, and if suitable facilities were provided, take two weeks of his ten on a real vacation. In one way or another, therefore, the average adult in this country could devote each year a period of about two weeks in doing the things of his own choice.

Here is an enormous undeveloped power—the spare time of our population. Suppose just one percent of it were focused on one particular job, such as increasing the facilities for the outdoor community life. This would be more than a million people, representing over two million weeks a year. It would be equivalent to 40,000 persons steadily on the job.

A Strategic Camping Base—The Appalachian Skyline

Where might this imposing force lay out its camping ground?

Camping grounds, of course, require wild lands. These in America are fortunately still available. They are in every main region of the country. They are the undeveloped or under-developed areas. Except in the Central States the wild lands now remaining are for the most part along the mountain ranges—the Sierras, the Cascades, and Rocky Mountains of the West and the Appalachian Mountains of the East.

Extensive national playgrounds have been reserved in various parts of the country for use by the people for camping and kindred purposes. Most of these are in the West where Uncle Sam's public lands were located. They are in the Yosemite, the Yellowstone, and many other National Parks—covering about six million acres in all. Splendid work has been accomplished in fitting these Parks for use. The National Forests, covering about 130 million acres—chiefly in the West—are also equipped for public recreation purposes.

A great public service has been started in these Parks and Forests in the field of outdoor life. They have been called "playgrounds of the people." This they are for the Western people—and those in the East who can afford time and funds for an extended trip in a Pullman car. But camping grounds to be of the most use to the people should be as near as possible to the center of the population. And this is in the East.

It fortunately happens that we have throughout the most densely populated portion of the United States a fairly continuous belt of under-developed lands. These are contained in the several ranges which form the Appalachian chain of mountains. Several National Forests have been purchased in this belt. These mountains, in several ways rivalling the western scenery, are within a day's ride from centers containing more than half the population of the United States. The region spans the climates of New England and the cotton belt; it contains the crops and the people of the North and of the South.

The skyline along the top of the main divides and ridges of the Appalachians would overlook a mighty part of the nation's activities. The rugged lands of this skyline would form a camping base strategic in the country's work and play.

Let us assume the existence of a giant standing high on the skyline along these mountain ridges, his head just scraping the floating clouds. What would he see from this skyline as he strode along its length from north to south?

Starting out from Mt. Washington, the highest point in the northeast, his horizon takes in one of the original happy hunting grounds of America—the "Northwoods," a country of pointed firs extending from the lakes and rivers of northern Maine to those of the Adirondacks. Stepping across the Green Mountains and the Berkshires to the Catskills he gets his first views of the crowded east—a chain of smoky bee-hive cities extending from Boston to Washington and containing a third of the population of the Appalachian drained area. Bridging the Delaware Water Gap and the Susquehanna on the picturesque Allegheny folds across Pennsylvania he notes more smoky columns—the big plants between Scranton and Pittsburgh that get out the basic stuff of modern industry—iron and coal. In relieving contrast he steps across the Potomac near Harpers Ferry and pushes through into the wooded wilderness of the Southern Appalachians where he finds preserved much of the primal aspects of the days of Daniel Boone. Here he finds, over on the Monongahela side, the black coal of bituminous and the white coal of water power. He proceeds along the great divide of the upper Ohio and sees flowing to waste, sometimes in terrifying floods, waters capable of generating untold hydroelectric energy and of bringing navigation to many a lower stream. He looks over the Natural Bridge and out across the battle fields around Appomattox. He finds himself finally in the midst of the great Carolina hardwood belt. Resting now on top of Mt. Mitchell, highest point east of the Rockies, he counts up on his big long fingers the opportunities which yet await development along the skyline he has passed.

First he notes the opportunities for recreation. Throughout the Southern Appalachians, throughout the Northwoods, and even through the Alleghenies that wind their way among the smoky industrial towns of Pennsylvania, he recollects vast areas of secluded forests, pastoral lands, and water courses, which, with proper facilities and protection, could be made to serve as the breath of a real life for the toilers in the bee-hive cities along the Atlantic seaboard and elsewhere.

Second, he notes the possibilities for health and recuperation. The oxygen in the mountain air along the Appalachian skyline is a natural resource (and a national resource) that radiates to the heavens its enormous health-giving powers with only a fraction of a percent utilized for human rehabilitation. Here is a resource that could save thousands of lives. The sufferers from tuberculosis, anemia, and insanity go through the whole strata of human society. Most of them are helpless, even those economically well off. They occur in the cities and right in the skyline belt. For the farmers, and especially the wives of farmers, are by no means escaping the grinding-down process of our modern life.

Most sanitariums now established are perfectly useless to those afflicted with mental disease—the most terrible, usually, of any disease. Many of these sufferers could be cured. But not merely by "treatment." They need comprehensive provision made for them. They need acres not medicine. Thousands of acres of this mountain land should be devoted to them with whole communities planned and equipped for their cure.

Next after the opportunities for recreation and recuperation our giant counts off, as a third big resource, the opportunities in the Appalachian belt for employment on the land. This brings up a need that is becoming urgent—the redistribution of our population, which grows more and more top heavy.

The rural population of the United States, and of the Eastern States adjacent to the Appalachians, has now dipped below the urban. For the whole country it has fallen from 60 per cent of the total in 1900 to 49 per cent in 1920; for the Eastern States it has fallen, during this period, from 55 per cent to 45 per cent. Meantime the per capita area of improved farm land has dropped, in the Eastern States, from 3.35 acres to 2.43 acres.

This is a shrinkage of nearly 18 percent in 20 years; in the States from Maine to Pennsylvania the shrinkage has been 40 per cent.

There are in the Appalachian belt probably 25 million acres of grazing and agricultural land awaiting development. Here is room for a whole new rural population. Here is an opportunity—if only the way can be found—for that counter migration from city to country that has so long been prayed for. But our giant in pondering on this resource is discerning enough to know that its utilization is going to depend upon some new deal in our agricultural system. This he knows if he ever stooped down and gazed in the sunken eyes of either the Carolina "cracker" or the Green Mountain "hayseed."

Forest land as well as agricultural might prove an opportunity for steady employment in the open. But this again depends upon a new deal. Forestry must replace timber devastation and its consequent hap-hazard employment. And this the giant knows if he has looked into the rugged face of the homeless "don't care a damn" lumberjack of the Northwoods.

Such are the outlooks—such the opportunities—seen by a discerning spirit from the Appalachian skyline.

Possibilities in the New Approach

Let's put up now to the wise and trained observer the particular question before us. What are the possibilities in the new approach to the problem of living? Would the development of the outdoor community life—as an offset and relief from the various shackles of commercial civilization—be practicable and worth while? From the experience of observations and thoughts along the sky-line here is a possible answer:

There are several possible gains from such an approach.

First there would be the "oxygen" that makes for a sensible optimism. Two weeks spent in the real open—right now, this year and next—would be a little real living for thousands of people which they would be sure of getting before they died. They would get a little fun as they went along regardless of problems being "solved." This would not damage the problems and it would help the folks.

Next there would be perspective. Life for two weeks on the mountain top would show up many things about life during the other fifty weeks down below. The latter could be viewed as a whole—away from its heat, sweat, and irritations. There would be a chance to catch a breath, to study the dynamic forces of nature and the possibilities of shifting to them the burdens now carried on the backs of men. The reposeful study of these forces should provide a broad gauged enlightened approach to the problems of industry. Industry would come to be seen in its true perspective—as a means in life and not an end in itself. The actual partaking of the recreative and non-industrial life—systematically by the people and not spasmodically by a few—should emphasize the distinction between it and the industrial life. It should stimulate the quest for enlarging the one and reducing the other. It should put new zest in the labor movement. Life and study of this kind should emphasize the need of going to the roots of industrial questions and avoiding superficial thinking and rash action. The problems of the farmer, the coal miner, and the lumberjack could be studied intimately and with minimum partiality. Such an approach should bring the poise that goes with understanding.

Finally, there would be new clues to constructive solutions. The organization of the cooperative camping life would tend to draw people out of the cities. Coming as visitors they would be loath to return. They would become desirous of settling down in the country—to work in the open as well as *play*. The various camps would require food. Why not raise the food, as well as consume it, on the cooperative plan? Food and farm camps should come about as a natural sequence. Timber is also required. Permanent small scale operations could be encouraged in the various Appalachian National Forests. The government now claims this is part of its forest policy. The camping life would stimulate forestry as well as better agriculture. Employment in both would tend to become enlarged.

How far these tendencies would go the wisest observer of course can not tell. They would have to be worked out step by step. But the tendencies at least would be established. They would be cutting channels leading to constructive achievement in the problem of living: they would be cutting across those now leading to destructive blindness.

A Project for Development

It looks, then, as if it might be worth while to devote some energy at least to working out a better utilization of our spare time. The spare time for one per cent of our population would be equivalent, as above reckoned, to the continuous activity of some 40,000 persons. If these people were on the skyline, and kept their eyes open, they would see the things that the giant could see. Indeed, this force of 40,000 would be a giant in itself. It could walk the skyline and develop its varied opportunities. And this is the job that we propose: a project to develop the opportunities—for recreation, recuperation, and employment—in the region of the Appalachian skyline.

The project is one for a series of recreational communities throughout the Appalachian chain of mountains from New England to Georgia, these to be connected by a walking trail. Its purpose is to establish a base for a more extensive and systematic development of outdoor community life. It is a project in housing and community architecture.

No scheme is proposed in this particular article for organizing or financing this project. Organizing is a matter of detail to be carefully worked out. Financing depends upon local public interest in the various localities affected.

Features of Project

There are four chief features of the Appalachian project:

1. *The Trail—*

The beginnings of an Appalachian trail already exist. They have been established for several years—in various localities along the line. Specially good work in trail building has been accomplished by the Appalachian Mountain Club in the White Mountains of New Hampshire and by the Green Mountain Club in Vermont. The latter association has built the "Long Trail" for 210 miles through the Green Mountains—four fifth of the distance from the Massachusetts line to the Canadian. Here is a project that will be logically extended. What the Green Mountains are to Vermont the Appalachians are to the eastern United States. What is suggested, therefore, is a "long trail" over the full length of the Appalachian skyline, from the highest peak in the north to the highest peak in the south—from Mt. Washington to Mt. Mitchell.

The trail should be divided into sections, each consisting preferably of the portion lying in a given State, or subdivision thereof. Each section should be in the immediate charge of a local group of people. Difficulties might arise over the use of private property—especially that amid agricultural lands on the crossovers between ranges. It might sometimes be necessary to obtain a State franchise for the use of rights of way. These matters could readily be adjusted, provided there is sufficient local interest in the project as a whole. The various sections should be under some form of general federated control, but no suggestions regarding this form are made in this article.

Not all of the trail within a section could, of course, be built at once. It would be a matter of several years. As far as possible the work undertaken for any one season should complete some definite usable link—as up or across one peak. Once completed it should be immediately opened for local use and not wait until the completion of other portions. Each portion built should, of course, be rigorously maintained and not allowed to revert to disuse. A trail is as serviceable as its poorest link.

The trail could be made, at each stage of its construction, of immediate strategic value in preventing and fighting forest fires. Lookout stations could be located at intervals along the way. A forest fire service could be organized in each section which should tie in with the services of the Federal and State governments. The trail would become immediately a battle line against fire.

A suggestion for the location of the trail and its main branches is shown in the accompanying map.

2. *Shelter Camps—*

These are the usual accompaniments of the trails which have been built in the White and Green Mountains. They are the trail's equipment for use. They should be located at convenient distances so as to allow a comfortable day's walk between each. They should be equipped always for sleeping and certain of them for serving meals—after the fashion of the Swiss chalets. Strict regulation is essential to provide that equipment is used and not abused. As far as possible the blazing and constructing of the trail and building of camps should be done by volunteer workers. For volunteer "work" is really "play." The spirit of cooperation, as usual in such enterprises, should be stimulated throughout. The enterprise should, of course, be conducted without profit. The trail must be well guarded against—the yegg-man, and against the profiteer.

3. *Community Camps*—

These would grow naturally out of the shelter camps and inns. Each would consist of a little community on or near the trail (perhaps on a neighboring lake) where people could live in private domiciles. Such a community might occupy a substantial area—perhaps a hundred acres or more. This should be bought and owned as part of the project. No separate lots should be sold therefrom. Each camp should be a self-owning community and not a real estate venture. The use of the separate domiciles, like all other features, should be available without profit.

These community camps should be carefully planned in advance. They should not be allowed to become too populous and thereby defeat the very purpose for which they are created. Greater numbers should be accommodated by *more* communities not *larger* ones. There is room, without crowding, in the Appalachian region for a very large camping population. The location of these community camps would form a main part of the regional planning and architecture.

These communities would be used for various kinds of non-industrial activity. They might eventually be organized for special purposes—for recreation, for recuperation, and for study. Summer schools or seasonal field courses could be established and scientific travel courses organized and accommodated in the different communities along the trail. The community camp should become something more than a mere "playground"; it should stimulate every possible line of outdoor non-industrial endeavor.

4. *Food and Farm Camps—*

These might not be organized at first. They would come as a later development. The farm camp is the natural supplement of the community camp. Here is the same spirit of cooperation and well ordered action the food and crops consumed in the outdoor living would as far as practicable be sown and harvested.

Food and farm camps could be established as special communities in adjoining valleys. Or they might be combined with the community camps by the inclusion of surrounding farm lands. Their development would provide a tangible opportunity for working out by actual experiment a fundamental matter in the problem of living. It would provide one definite avenue of experiment in getting "back to the land." It would provide an opportunity for those anxious to settle down in the country; it would open up a possible source for new, and needed, employment. Communities of this type are illustrated by the Hudson Guild Farm in New Jersey.

Fuelwood, logs, and lumber are other basic needs of the camps and communities along the trail. These also might be grown and forested as part of the camp activity, rather than bought in the lumber market. The nucleus of such an enterprise has already been started at Camp Tamiment, Pennsylvania, on a lake not far from the proposed route of the Appalachian trail. This camp has been established by a labor group in New York City. They have erected a sawmill on their tract of 2000 acres and have built the bungalows of their community from their own timber.

Farm camps might ultimately be supplemented by permanent forest camps through the acquisition (or lease) of wood and timber tracts. These of course should be handled under a system of forestry so as to have a continuously growing crop of material. The object sought might be accomplished through long term timber sale contracts with the Federal Government on some of the Appalachian National Forests. Here would be another opportunity for permanent, steady, healthy employment in the open.

Elements of Dramatic Appeal

The results achievable in the camp and scouting life are common knowl-edge to all who have passed the tenderfoot stage therein. The camp community is a sanctuary and a refuge from the scramble of every-day worldly commercial life. It is in essence a retreat from profit. Cooperation replaces antagonism, trust replaces suspicion, emulation replaces compe-tition. An Appalachian trail, with its camps, communities, and spheres of influence along the skyline, should, with reasonably good management, accomplish these achievements. And they possess within them the ele-ments of a deep dramatic appeal.

Indeed the lure of the scouting life can be made the most formidable enemy of the lure of militarism (a thing with which this country is men-aced along with all others). It comes the nearest perhaps, of things thus far protected, to supplying what Professor James once called a "moral equivalent of war." It appeals to the primal instincts of a fighting heroism, of volunteer service and of work in a common cause.

These instincts are pent up forces in every human and they demand their outlet. This is the avowed object of the boy scout or girl scout move-ment, but it should not be limited to juveniles.

The building and protection of an Appalachian trail, with its various communities, interests, and possibilities, would form at least one outlet. Here is a job for 40,000 souls. This trail could be made to be, in a very literal sense, a battle line against fire and flood—and even against dis-ease. Such battles—against the common enemies of man—still lack, it is true, the "punch" of man vs. man. There is but one reason—publicity. Militarism has been made colorful in a world of drab. But the care of the country side, which the scouting life instills, is vital in any real protection of "home and country." Already basic it can be made spectacular. Here is something to be dramatized.

2: INVITATION TO JOIN THE WILDERNESS SOCIETY

The following invitation was sent by the four conceivers of the Wilderness Society to six influential colleagues they hoped would join them as founding members. The letter was sent to H. C. (Harold) Anderson, John Collier, Aldo Leopold, John C. Merriam, Ernest Oberholtzer, and Robert Sterling Yard. Only Collier and Merriam declined.

Washington, D.C.

October 19, 1934

We, the undersigned, have constituted ourselves a committee to take the steps necessary to organize an aggressive society for the preservation of the wilderness. We are asking you and five others whose names appear at the end of this letter to join with us as an organizing committee of ten. We desire to integrate the growing sentiment which we believe exists in this country for holding its wild areas *sound-proof* as well as *sight-proof* from our increasingly mechanized life. We believe that the following principles should be considered basic in the proposed organization.

1. That the wilderness (the environment of solitude) is a natural mental resource having the same basic relation to man's ultimate thought and culture as coal, timber, and other physical resources have to his material side.

2. That the time has come, with the brutalizing pressure of a spreading metropolitan civilization, to recognize this wilderness environment as a serious human need rather than a luxury and plaything.

3. That this need is being sacrificed by the metropolitan invasion in its various killing forms, of which the worst are the *motor road* and *radio.*

4. That scenery and solitude are intrinsically separate things, that the motorist is entitled to his full share of scenery, but that motorway and solitude together constitute a contradiction.

5. That outing areas in which people may enjoy the now-primitive forest are highly desirable for many pent-up city people who have

no desire for solitude, but that such areas should not be combined with those reserved for the wilderness.

6. That the wilderness remaining in America has shrunk to such a small remnant of the country's total territory, that what area does remain is all-precious and its preservation constitutes a vital necessity.

7. That encroachment upon our remnant American wilderness in any one locality is an attack upon the whole and creates therefore an issue of national moment and not one for local action alone.

8. That since the invasion of wilderness areas is generally boosted by powerful, country-wide organizations, it is essential that individuals and groups who desire to preserve the wilderness must unite in a country-wide movement in its defense.

9. That the thoughts above noted are shared by an increasing proportion of American people, but that effective action depends on focusing the strength of their united wills.

Therefore, we are proposing the immediate formation of a group to be called *The Wilderness Society* for the purpose of determining what are the wilderness areas which should be preserved, and for saving them from destruction.

Will you join us as organizers of such a society?
Signed,
Robert Marshall
Harvey Broome
Benton MacKaye
Bernard Frank[1]

3: Excerpts from the Wilderness Act

The Wilderness Act of 1964 designated 9.1 million acres in thirteen states as wilderness. Today, there are 803 wilderness areas (111,696,927 acres) located in forty-four states and Puerto Rico. The amount of designated wilderness is about 5 percent of America's total. Because over half of the wilderness areas are in Alaska, the amount of designated wilderness in the contiguous states is around 2.7 percent—an area about the size of Minnesota.[1]

Written by Howard Zahniser and refined through countless meetings and revision cycles, the Wilderness Act stands as his greatest gift and legacy.

AN ACT
To establish a National Wilderness Preservation System for the permanent good of the whole people, and for other purposes.
SECTION 1. This Act may be cited as the "Wilderness Act."
WILDERNESS SYSTEM ESTABLISHED STATEMENT OF POLICY
SECTION 2. In order to assure that an increasing population, accompanied by expanding settlement and growing mechanization, does not occupy and modify all areas within the United States and its possessions, leaving no lands designated for preservation and protection in their natural condition, it is hereby declared to be the policy of the Congress to secure for the American people of present and future generations the benefits of an enduring resource of wilderness. For this purpose there is hereby established a National Wilderness Preservation System to be composed of federally owned areas designated by Congress as "wilderness areas," and these shall be administered for the use and enjoyment of the American people in such manner as will leave them unimpaired for future use and enjoyment as wilderness, and so as to provide for the protection of these areas, the preservation of their wilderness character, and for the gathering and dissemination of information regarding their use and enjoyment as wilderness; and no Federal lands shall be designated as "wilderness areas" except as provided for in this Act or by a subsequent Act.

DEFINITION OF WILDERNESS

A wilderness, in contrast with those areas where man and his works dominate the landscape, is hereby recognized as an area where the earth and its community of life are untrammeled by man, where man himself is a visitor who does not remain. An area of wilderness is further defined to mean in this Act an area of undeveloped Federal land retaining its primeval character and influence, without permanent improvements or human habitation, which is protected and managed so as to preserve its natural conditions and which (1) generally appears to have been affected primarily by the forces of nature, with the imprint of man's work substantially unnoticeable; (2) has outstanding opportunities for solitude or a primitive and unconfined type of recreation; (3) has at least five thousand acres of land or is of sufficient size as to make practicable its preservation and use in an unimpaired condition; and (4) may also contain ecological, geological, or other features of scientific, educational, scenic, or historical value.

PROHIBITION OF CERTAIN USES

Except as specifically provided for in this Act, and subject to existing private rights, there shall be no commercial enterprise and no permanent road within any wilderness area designated by this Act and except as necessary to meet minimum requirements for the administration of the area for the purpose of this Act (including measures required in emergencies involving the health and safety of persons within the area), there shall be no temporary road, no use of motor vehicles, motorized equipment or motorboats, no landing of aircraft, no other form of mechanical transport, and no structure or installation within any such area.[2]

BIBLIOGRAPHY

Albright, Horace M., and Marian Albright Schenck. *Creating the National Park Service: The Missing Years.* Norman: University of Oklahoma Press. 1999.

Anderson, Larry. *Benton MacKaye: Conservationist, Planner, and Creator of the Appalachian Trail.* Baltimore: Johns Hopkins University Press, 2002.

Beveridge, Charles E., ed. *Frederick Law Olmsted: Writings on Landscape, Culture and Society.* New York: Library of America, 2015.

Bowles, Samuel. *Across the Continent: A Summer's Journey to the Rocky Mountains, the Mormons and the Pacific States with Speaker Colfax.* Springfield, MA: Samuel Bowles; New York: Hurd and Houghton, 1865.

Broome, Harvey. *Faces of the Wilderness.* Missoula, MT: Mountain Press, 1972.

Cornell, Alonzo B. *Public Papers of Alonzo B. Cornell, Governor of the State of New York.* Albany, NY: E. H. Bender, 1882.

Cosco, Jon N. *Echo Park: Struggle for Preservation.* Boulder, CO: Johnson Books, 1995.

Cox, Francis M., ed. *The Abridgment. Message from the President of the United States to the Two Houses of Congress at the Beginning of the Second Session of the Fifty-Third Congress, with the Reports of the Heads of Departments and Selections from Accompanying Documents.* Washington, DC: U.S. Government Printing Office, 1894.

Gardiner, James T. (and Frederick Law Olmsted). *Special Report of New York State Survey on the Preservation of the Scenery of Niagara Falls, and Fourth Annual Report on the Triangulation of the State for the Year 1879.* Albany, NY: Charles Van Benthuysen, 1880.

Gaston, Bibi. *Gifford Pinchot and the First Foresters: The Untold Story of the Brave Men and Women Who Launched the American Conservation Movement.* New Milford, CT: Baked Apple Club, 2016.

Gilliam, Ann, ed. *Voices for the Earth: A Treasury of the Sierra Club Bulletin, 1897–1977.* San Francisco, Sierra Club Books, 1979.

Glover, James M. *A Wilderness Original: The Life of Bob Marshall.* Seattle: Mountaineers, 1986.

Gove, Bill. *J. E. Henry's Logging Railroads.* Littleton, NH: Bondcliff Books, 1998.

Harvey, Mark, ed. *The Wilderness Writings of Howard Zahniser.* Seattle: University of Washington Press, 2014.

Hough, Franklin B. *Report upon Forestry: Prepared under the Direction of the Commissioner of Agriculture, in Pursuance of an Act of Congress Approved August 15, 1876.* Washington, DC: U.S. Government Printing Office, 1878.

Johnson, Christopher, and David Govatski. *Forests for the People: The Story of America's Eastern National Forests*. Washington, DC: Island Press, 2013.

Jones, Holway R. *John Muir and the Sierra Club: The Battle for Yosemite*. San Francisco: Sierra Club, 1965.

Lewis, James G., and Marcia Spencer. *Pisgah National Forest: A History*. Charleston, SC: History Press, 2014.

MacKaye, Benton. *Expedition Nine: A Return to a Region*. Washington, DC: Wilderness Society, 1969.

MacKaye, Percy. *Epoch: The Life of Steele MacKaye, Genius of the Theatre in Relation to his Contemporaries*. Vol. 2. New York: Boni and Liveright, 1927.

Martin, Justin. *Genius of Place: The Life of Frederick Law Olmsted*. Boston: Da Capo, 2011.

McGeary, M. Nelson. *Gifford Pinchot: Forester-Politician*. Princeton, NJ: Princeton University Press, 1960.

Miller, Char. *Gifford Pinchot and the Making of Modern Environmentalism*. Washington, DC: Island Press, 2001.

Morison, Elting Elmore, ed. *The Letters of Theodore Roosevelt: The Years of Preparation, 1868–1900*. Vol. 2, *1898–1900*. Cambridge, MA: Harvard University Press, 1951.

Nash, Roderick Frazier. *Wilderness and the American Mind*. 5th ed. New Haven, CT: Yale University Press, 2001.

Paddock, Joe. *Keeper of the Wild: The Life of Ernest Oberholtzer*. St. Paul: Minnesota Historical Society Press, 2001.

Pinchot, Gifford. *Breaking New Ground*. 1947. Reprint, Seattle: University of Washington Press, Americana Library Edition, 1972.

Pinkett, Harold T. *Gifford Pinchot, Private and Public Forester*. Chicago: University of Illinois Press, 1970.

Quinn, Arthur Hobson. *Representative American Plays*. New York: Century Co., 1921.

Roper, Laura Wood. *FLO: A Biography of Frederic Law Olmsted*. Baltimore: Johns Hopkins University Press, 1973.

Rybcznski, Witold. *A Clearing in the Distance: Frederick Law Olmsted and America in the 19th Century*. New York: Scribner, 1999.

Schenck, Carl Alwin, and Ovid Butler. *Cradle of Forestry in America: The Biltmore Forest School, 1898–1913*. Durham, NC: Forest History Society, 1998.

Scott, Doug. *The Enduring Wilderness*. Golden, CO: Fulcrum, 2004.

Stevenson, Elizabeth. *Park Maker: A Life of Frederick Law Olmsted*. New Brunswick, NJ: Transaction, 2000.

Sutter, Paul. *Driven Wild: How the Fight against Automobiles Launched the Modern Wilderness Movement*. Seattle: University of Washington Press, 2002.

Terrie, Philip G. *Forever Wild: A Cultural History of Wilderness in the Adirondacks*. New York: Syracuse University Press. 1994.

Turner, Tom. *David Brower: The Making of an Environmental Movement*. Oakland: University of California Press, 2015.

USDA. "Forest Preservation and National Prosperity. Portions of Addresses Delivered at the American Forest Congress, January 2 to 6, 1905, by President Roosevelt, Ambassador Jusserand, Secretary Wilson, and Others." Circular No. 35.

USDA Division of Forestry. *Report of the Forester, 1899*. Washington, DC.

NOTES

PREFACE

1. Frederick Law Olmsted to Mariana Griswold Van Rensselaer, June 18, 1893, in *Frederick Law Olmsted: Writings on Landscape, Culture and Society*, ed. Charles E. Beveridge (New York: Library of America, 2015), loc. 12157, Kindle.

CHAPTER 1: FREDERICK LAW OLMSTED'S EPIPHANY

1. Laura Wood Roper, *FLO: A Biography of Frederic Law Olmsted* (Baltimore: Johns Hopkins University Press, 1973), 245.

2. Roper, *FLO: A Biography*, 245.

3. Frederick Law Olmsted to Frederick N. Knapp, November 22, 1863, Frederick Law Olmsted Papers: Speeches and Writings File, Library of Congress.

4. Frederick Law Olmsted to George W. Farlee, November 14, 1863, Mariposa Letter Book, 27, 103, Frederick Law Olmsted Papers: Speeches and Writings File, Library of Congress.

5. Frederick Law Olmsted to Mary Cleveland Perkins Olmsted, November 20, 1863, image 2 of Frederick Law Olmsted Papers: Subject File, 1857–1952, Parks, Yosemite Valley, California, 1863–1891, https://www.loc.gov/resource/mss35121.mss35121_037 _0386_0553/?sp=2&r=-0.23,-0.066,1.037,0.493,0.

6. Witold Rybcznski, *A Clearing in the Distance: Frederick Law Olmsted and America in the 19th Century* (New York: Scribner, 1999), 235.

7. Frederick Law Olmsted to John Olmsted, August 17, 1864, image 3 of Frederick Law Olmsted Papers: Subject File, 1857–1952, Parks, Yosemite Valley, California, 1863–1891, https://www.loc.gov/resource/mss35121.mss35121_037_0386_0553/?sp =2&r=0.009,0.079,0.622,0.295,0.

8. Justin Martin, *Genius of Place: The Life of Frederick Law Olmsted* (Boston: Da Capo, 2011), 246.

9. Elizabeth Stevenson, *Park Maker: A Life of Frederick Law Olmsted* (New Brunswick, NJ: Transaction, 2000), 271.

10. Stevenson, *Park Maker*, 271.

11. Charles E. Beveridge, ed., *Frederick Law Olmsted: Writings on Landscape, Culture and Society* (New York: Library of America, 2015), loc. 5474, Kindle.

12. Frederick Law Olmsted, "The Yosemite Valley and the Mariposa Big Trees: A Preliminary Report," 1865, with an introductory note by Laura Wood Roper, repr. from *Landscape Architecture* 43, no. 1 (October, 1952): 22.

13. *Encyclopedia Britannica*, 11th ed. (1911), s.v. "Samuel Bowles III."
14. Samuel Bowles, *Across the Continent: A Summer's Journey to the Rocky Mountains, the Mormons and the Pacific States with Speaker Colfax* (Springfield, MA: Samuel Bowles and Co.; New York: Hurd and Houghton, 1865), 223.
15. Charles E. Beveridge, "Olmsted and Yosemite," Foundation for Landscape Studies, *SiteLINES: A Journal of Place*, vol. 5, no. 1 (2009): 6–8, http://www.jstor.org/stable/24889349.
16. Bowles, *Across the Continent*, 231.
17. Roper, *FLO: A Biography*, 291.
18. Beveridge, "Olmsted and Yosemite."
19. David Brower, foreword to "Yosemite: The Story of an Idea," *Sierra Club Bulletin* 33, no. 3 (March 1948): 47.
20. Hans Huth, "Yosemite: The Story of an Idea," *Sierra Club Bulletin* 33, no. 3 (March 1948): 47.
21. Frederick Law Olmsted, "The Yosemite Valley and the Mariposa Big Tree Grove," 1865, in *America's National Park System: The Critical Documents*, chap. 1, "The Early Years, 1864–1918," accessed October 12, 2021, https://www.nps.gov/parkhistory/online_books/anps/anps_1b.htm.
22. Huth, "Yosemite: The Story of an Idea," 47.
23. Olmsted, "The Yosemite Valley and the Mariposa Big Tree Grove."

CHAPTER 2: HAPPILY ASSOCIATED PASSAGES OF AMERICAN SCENERY

1. Justin Martin, *Genius of Place: The Life of Frederick Law Olmsted* (Boston: Da Capo, 2011), 109.
2. Witold Rybczynski, *A Clearing in the Distance: Frederick Law Olmsted and America in the 19th Century* (New York: Scribner, 1999), 162.
3. Olmsted and Vaux (firm), *Description of a Plan for the Improvement of Central Park: "Greensward,"* New York, 1858, 8.
4. Olmsted and Vaux, *Description of a Plan*, 18.
5. Charles E. Beveridge, *The Distinctive Charms of the Niagara Scenery: Frederick Law Olmsted and the Niagara Reservation* (catalog for the 1985 Niagara Reservation art exhibit), accessed March 8, 2021, https://buffaloah.com/h/bev.
6. Beveridge, *Distinctive Charms*.
7. Elizabeth Stevenson, *Park Maker: A Life of Frederick Law Olmsted* (New Brunswick, NJ: Transaction, 2000), 191.
8. Laura Wood Roper, *FLO: A Biography of Frederic Law Olmsted* (Baltimore: Johns Hopkins University Press, 1973), 154.
9. Library of Congress, Image 28 of Frederick Law Olmsted Papers: Correspondence, 1838–1928; General Correspondence, 1838–1928; 1865, March–April, https://www.loc.gov/resource/mss35121.mss35121_009_0169_0259/?sp=28&r=-0.72,0.039,2.441,1.137,0.
10. Beveridge, *Distinctive Charms*.
11. Frederick Law Olmsted to C. K. Remington, May 28, 1888, Olmsted Papers, Manuscript Division, Library of Congress.
12. James T. Gardiner (and Frederick Law Olmsted), *Special Report of New York State Survey on the Preservation of the Scenery of Niagara Falls, and Fourth Annual Report on*

the Triangulation of the State for the Year 1879 (Albany, NY: Charles Van Benthuysen, 1880), 7.

13. Gardiner and Olmsted, *Special Report*, 7.

14. Gardiner and Olmsted, *Special Report*, 10.

15. Gardiner and Olmsted, *Special Report*, 9–10.

16. Gardiner and Olmsted, *Special Report*, 15–16.

17. P. M. Eckel, *Olmsted, Yosemite and the Niagara Reservation*, Res Botanica, Missouri Botanical Garden, July 22, 2003, accessed March 10, 2021, http://www.mobot.org/plant science/ResBot/Niag/Hist2/Olmsted.htm.

CHAPTER 3: THE BIRTHPLACE OF AMERICAN FORESTRY

1. Elizabeth Stevenson, *Park Maker: A Life of Frederick Law Olmsted* (New Brunswick, NJ: Transaction, 2000), 387.

2. Stevenson, *Park Maker*, 389.

3. Justin Martin, *Genius of Place: The Life of Frederick Law Olmsted* (Boston: Da Capo, 2011), 361.

4. Martin, *Genius of Place*, 362.

5. Char Miller, *Gifford Pinchot and the Making of Modern Environmentalism* (Washington, DC: Island Press, 2001), 57.

6. M. Nelson McGeary, *Gifford Pinchot: Forester-Politician* (Princeton, NJ: Princeton University Press, 1960), 15–16.

7. USDA Forest Service website, accessed March 15, 2021, https://www.fs.usda.gov /detail/greytowers/aboutgreytowers/history/?cid=stelprd3824502.

8. Miller, *Gifford Pinchot*, 105.

CHAPTER 4: TRIUMPH AND TRAGEDY

1. Memorandum from Frederick Law Olmsted to Chicago Exposition Commissioners, March 1891, in *Frederick Law Olmsted: Writings on Landscape, Culture and Society*, ed. Charles E. Beveridge (New York: Library of America, 2015), loc. 11850, Kindle.

2. Memorandum from Frederick Law Olmsted to Chicago Exposition Commissioners.

3. Justin Martin, *Genius of Place: The Life of Frederick Law Olmsted* (Boston: Da Capo, 2011), 386.

4. Martin, *Genius of Place*, 382.

5. United States Census Bureau, *U.S. Census Bureau History: 1893 Chicago World's Fair*, accessed March 18, 2021, https://www.census.gov/history/www/homepage_archive /2018/may_2018.html.

6. U.S. Census Bureau, *1893 Chicago World's Fair*.

7. Judith A. Adams, "The Promotion of New Technology through Fun and Spectacle: Electricity at the World's Columbian Exposition," *Journal of American Culture* 18, no. 2 (1995): 45–55, accessed March 18, 2013, http://dx.doi.org/10.1111/j.1542-734X.1995 .00045.x.

8. Daniel Burnham, "White City and Capital City," *Century Illustrated* 63, no. 4 (1902): 619.

9. Scott McQuire, *The Media City: Media, Architecture and Urban Space* (Los Angeles: Sage, 2008), 35.

10. Percy MacKaye, *Epoch: The Life of Steele MacKaye, Genius of the Theatre in Relation to His Contemporaries*, vol. 2 (New York: Boni and Liveright, 1927), 314.
11. "Buffalo's Steele MacKaye, the 'Father of Modern Acting,'" *Buffalo History Gazette*, June 16, 2011, accessed March 19, 2021, https://www.buffalohistorygazette.net/2011/06.
12. Arthur Hobson Quinn, *Representative American Plays* (New York: Century Co., 1921), 495.
13. James Fisher, *Historical Dictionary of American Theater: Beginnings* (Lanham, MD: Rowman & Littlefield, 2015).
14. Christopher Benfey, *If: The Untold Story of Kipling's American Years* (New York: Penguin, 2019), 82.
15. Percy MacKaye, *Epoch*, vii.
16. "Buffalo's Steele MacKaye."
17. Illinois Historical Art Project, "The Columbian Exposition and the Spectatorium," accessed March 21, 2021, https://www.illinoisart.org/spectatorium-1893worlds-fair.
18. Percy MacKaye, *Epoch*, 306.
19. Percy MacKaye, *Epoch*, 301.
20. Percy MacKaye, *Epoch*, 301.
21. Percy MacKaye, *Epoch*, 312.
22. "Buffalo's Steele MacKaye."
23. Percy MacKaye, *Epoch*, 345–47.
24. Percy MacKaye, *Epoch*, 353.
25. Percy MacKaye, *Epoch*, 379.
26. Percy MacKaye, *Epoch*, 399.
27. Percy MacKaye, *Epoch*, 406 (quote attributed to *Chicago Times* article of June 4, 1893).
28. Percy MacKaye, *Epoch*, 406 (quote attributed to *Chicago Times* article of June 4, 1893).
29. Percy MacKaye, *Epoch*, 423.
30. Percy MacKaye, *Epoch*, 425.
31. Percy MacKaye, *Epoch*, 426 (quote attributed to Steele MacKaye friend Moses P. Handy from his article in *Chicago Inter-Ocean* of February 27, 1894).

CHAPTER 5: PASSING THE BATON
1. Frederick Law Olmsted to Henry Van Brunt, January 22, 1891, in *Frederick Law Olmsted: Writings on Landscape, Culture and Society*, ed. Charles E. Beveridge (New York: Library of America, 2015), loc. 11786, Kindle.
2. Frederick Law Olmsted to Mariana Griswold Van Rensselaer, June 18, 1893, in Beveridge, *Frederick Law Olmsted: Writings on Landscape, Culture and Society*, loc. 12157.
3. Gifford Pinchot, *Breaking New Ground* (1947; repr., Seattle: University of Washington Press, Americana Library Edition, 1972), 21.
4. Gifford Pinchot, *Breaking New Ground*, 21.
5. Gifford Pinchot, *Breaking New Ground*, 23.
6. Gifford Pinchot, *Breaking New Ground*, 49.
7. Gifford Pinchot, *Breaking New Ground*, 70.
8. Gifford Pinchot, *Breaking New Ground*, 70.

CHAPTER 6: CREATING FERTILE GROUND

1. Arthur A. Ekirch, "Franklin B. Hough: First Citizen of the Adirondacks," *Environmental Review* 7, no. 3 (1983): 271–74, accessed April 12, 2021, http://doi:10.2307/3984484.
2. Ekirch, "First Citizen."
3. Ekirch, "First Citizen."
4. Franklin B. Hough, "On the Duty of Governments in the Preservation of Forests" (from the Proceedings of the American Association for the Advancement of Science, Portland Meeting, August 1873), Library of Congress, accessed April 12, 2021, http://memory.loc.gov/cgi-bin/ampage?collId=amrvg&fileName=vg28//amrvgvg28.db&recNum=2&itemLink=r?ammem/consrvbib:@FIELD(NUMBER(vg28))&linkText=0.
5. Franklin B. Hough, *Report upon Forestry: Prepared under the Direction of the Commissioner of Agriculture, in Pursuance of an Act of Congress Approved August 15, 1876* (Washington, DC: U.S. Government Printing Office, 1878), 16.
6. New York State Library, "Biographical Note: Franklin Benjamin Hough," accessed April 13, 2021, http://www.nysl.nysed.gov/msscfa/sc7009.htm.
7. Ekirch, "First Citizen."
8. New York State Library, *Biographical Note: Franklin Benjamin Hough.*
9. Char Miller, "Amateur Hour: Nathaniel H. Egleston and Professional Forestry in Post-Civil War America," *Forest History Today*, Spring/Fall 2005, 20.
10. Gifford Pinchot, *Breaking New Ground* (1947; repr., Seattle: University of Washington Press Americana Library, 1972), 135.
11. M. Nelson McGeary, *Gifford Pinchot: Forester-Politician* (Princeton, NJ: Princeton University Press, 1960), 25.
12. McGeary, *Gifford Pinchot*, 27.

CHAPTER 7: MAKING THE PUSH

1. Gifford Pinchot, *Breaking New Ground* (1947; repr., Seattle: University of Washington Press, Americana Library Edition, 1972), 29.
2. Gifford Pinchot, *Breaking New Ground*, 29.
3. Gifford Pinchot, *Breaking New Ground*, 29.
4. Gifford Pinchot, *Breaking New Ground*, 9.
5. Gifford Pinchot, *Breaking New Ground*, 49–50.
6. Phyllis Anderson. "'Master of a Felicitous English Style': William Augustus Stiles, Editor of *Garden and Forest*," accessed April 7, 2021, https://www.loc.gov/preservation/about/prd/gardfor/essays/andersen.html.
7. Shen Hou, "*Garden and Forest*: A Forgotten Magazine and the Urban Roots of American Environmentalism," *Environmental History* 17, no. 4 (2012): 813–42, accessed April 7, 2021, http://www.jstor.org/stable/41721446.
8. Hou, "*Garden and Forest*."
9. Gifford Pinchot, "The Forest—The Sihlwald.—1," *Garden and Forest*, July 30, 1890, 374.
10. Gifford Pinchot, *Breaking New Ground*, 33.

CHAPTER 8: BENTON FINDS HIS WAY

1. Larry Anderson, *Benton MacKaye: Conservationist, Planner, and Creator of the Appalachian Trail* (Baltimore: Johns Hopkins University Press, 2002), 21.
2. Percy MacKaye, *Epoch: The Life of Steele MacKaye, Genius of the Theatre in Relation to His Contemporaries*, vol. 2 (New York: Boni and Liveright, 1927), 169.
3. Percy MacKaye, *Epoch*, 169.
4. Benton MacKaye, *Expedition Nine: A Return to a Region* (Washington, DC: Wilderness Society, 1969), 1–2.

CHAPTER 9: FACING THE HEADWINDS OF CHANGE

1. Gifford Pinchot, *Breaking New Ground* (1947; repr., Seattle: University of Washington Press, Americana Library Edition, 1972), 84.
2. Carl Schurz, "The Need of a Rational Forest Policy in the United States" (address delivered before the American Forestry Association and the Pennsylvania Forestry Association, October 15, 1889), 4.
3. Schurz, "The Need of a Rational Forest Policy," 5.
4. Schurz, "The Need of a Rational Forest Policy," 5.
5. Schurz, "The Need of a Rational Forest Policy," 6.
6. Schurz, "The Need of a Rational Forest Policy," 11–12.
7. Gifford Pinchot, *Breaking New Ground*, 85.
8. Gifford Pinchot, *Breaking New Ground*, 85–86.

CHAPTER 10: THE ADIRONDACKS STIR DEBATE

1. Alonzo B. Cornell, *Public Papers of Alonzo B. Cornell, Governor of the State of New York* (Albany, NY: E. H. Bender, 1882), 44.
2. Cornell, *Public Papers*, 44.
3. Commissioners of State Parks of New York, *First Annual Report of the Commissioners of State Parks of New York*, New York State Doc. No. 102, May 15, 1873, 9–10.
4. Commissioners of State Parks of New York, *First Annual Report*, 13–14.
5. Senate of New York, *Report of the Special Committee on State Lands in the Adirondack Region*, New York State Doc. No. 23, 1884, 13.
6. Louise A. Halper, "'A Rich Man's Paradise': Constitutional Preservation of New York State's Adirondack Forest, a Centenary Consideration," *Ecology Law Quarterly* 19, no. 2 (1992): 193–267, accessed April 22, 2021, http://www.jstor.org/stable/24113132.
7. Halper, "A Rich Man's Paradise," 193–267.
8. Philip G. Terrie, *Forever Wild: A Cultural History of Wilderness in the Adirondacks* (New York: Syracuse University Press, 1994), 98.
9. Terrie, *Forever Wild*, 99.
10. Gifford Pinchot, *Breaking New Ground*, 27.

CHAPTER 11: A FORESTER WITHOUT FORESTS

1. Gifford Pinchot, *Breaking New Ground* (1947; repr., Seattle: University of Washington Press, Americana Library Edition, 1972), 86.
2. Gifford Pinchot, *Breaking New Ground*, 86.

3. Gifford Pinchot, *Breaking New Ground*, 87.

4. National Academy of Sciences, "Moments in Academy History: Wolcott Gibbs," accessed April 29, 2021, http://www.nasonline.org/about-nas/history/highlights/wolcott -gibbs.html.

5. Gifford Pinchot, *Breaking New Ground*, 88.

6. Francis M. Cox, ed., *The Abridgment. Message from the President of the United States to the Two Houses of Congress at the Beginning of the Second Session of the Fifty-Third Congress, with the Reports of the Heads of Departments and Selections from Accompanying Documents* (Washington, DC: U.S. Government Printing Office, 1894), 28.

7. Gifford Pinchot, *Breaking New Ground*, 94.

8. Gifford Pinchot, *Breaking New Ground*, 92.

9. Gifford Pinchot, *Breaking New Ground*, 100.

10. Gifford Pinchot, *Breaking New Ground*, 103.

11. Gifford Pinchot, *Breaking New Ground*, 106.

12. Gifford Pinchot, *Breaking New Ground*, 108.

13. Gifford Pinchot, *Breaking New Ground*, 108.

14. Robert Bassman, "The 1897 Organic Act: A Historical Perspective," *Natural Resources Lawyer* 7, no. 3 (1974): 509, accessed May 3, 2021, http://www.jstor.org /stable/40922334.

15. Gifford Pinchot, *Breaking New Ground*, 115.

16. Gifford Pinchot, *Breaking New Ground*, 119.

17. Organic Act of 1897, Pub. L. No. 2, § 24 of 26 Stat. 1095 (March 3, 1891), 2.

18. Gifford Pinchot, *Breaking New Ground*, 120.

19. M. Nelson McGeary, *Gifford Pinchot: Forester-Politician* (Princeton, NJ: Princeton University Press, 1960), 42.

20. Gifford Pinchot, *Breaking New Ground*, 131.

CHAPTER 12: FORESTER FOR LIFE

1. Gifford Pinchot, *Breaking New Ground* (1947; repr., Seattle: University of Washington Press, Americana Library Edition, 1972), 137.

2. Gifford Pinchot, *Breaking New Ground*, 133–35.

3. Harold T. Pinkett, *Gifford Pinchot, Private and Public Forester* (Chicago: University of Illinois Press, 1970), 48.

4. Gifford Pinchot, *Breaking New Ground*, 141.

5. USDA Division of Forestry, *Report of the Forester, 1899*, Washington, DC, 3–4.

6. Gifford Pinchot, *Breaking New Ground*, 142.

7. Pinkett, *Gifford Pinchot*, 51.

8. Ralph S. Hosmer, interview by Elwood R. Maunder, September 26, 1960, Forest History Society, 6, https://foresthistory.org/wp-content/uploads/2016/12/HOSMER60 .pdf.

9. Ralph S. Hosmer, "Some Recollections of Gifford Pinchot, 1898–1904," *Journal of Forestry* 43 (August 1945): 560.

10. Ralph S. Hosmer, interview.

11. Pinkett, *Gifford Pinchot*, 50.

Chapter 13: A Profession Takes Root

1. Carl Schurz, "The Need of a Rational Forest Policy in the United States" (address delivered before the American Forestry Association and the Pennsylvania Forestry Association, October 15, 1889), 11.

2. Carl Alwin Schenck and Ovid Butler, *Cradle of Forestry in America: The Biltmore Forest School, 1898–1913* (Durham, NC: Forest History Society, 1998), 29–44.

3. Schenck and Butler, *Cradle of Forestry*, 50.

4. James G. Lewis and Marcia Spencer, *Pisgah National Forest: A History* (Charleston, SC: History Press, 2014), 61.

5. Schenck and Butler, *Cradle of Forestry*, 164.

6. Caption from Forest History Society Photo Collection, accessed May 5, 2021, https://foresthistory.org/november-26-1908-the-biltmore-forest-fair.

7. Southern Lumberman, *Forest Festival at Biltmore Estate* (Montgomery, AL: Hatton-Brown, 1908), 27.

8. Forest History Society and Cradle of Forestry in America Interpretive Association, producers, *First in Forestry: Carl Schenck and the Biltmore Forest School* (Asheville, NC: Bonesteel Films, 2015).

9. Carl Alwin Schenck, *Biltmore Doings*, January 1914, 1.

10. Kenneth H. Hayward, "The Fox and the Forest," *The Conservationist*, magazine of New York State's Department of Environmental Conservation, January–February, 1988, 3.

11. James Lassoie, Raymond Ogelesby, and Peter Smallidge, "Roots of American Forestry Education: Trials and Tribulations at Cornell University," *Forest History Today*, 1998, 22.

12. Louise A. Halper, "'A Rich Man's Paradise': Constitutional Preservation of New York State's Adirondack Forest, a Centenary Consideration," *Ecology Law Quarterly* 19, no. 2 (1992): 233, accessed May 6, 2021, http://www.jstor.org/stable/24113132.

13. Gifford Pinchot, *Breaking New Ground* (1947; repr., Seattle: University of Washington Press, Americana Library Edition, 1972), 136.

14. Ralph S. Hosmer, interview by Elwood R. Maunder, September 26, 1960, Forest History Society, 13, https://foresthistory.org/wp-content/uploads/2016/12/HOSMER60.pdf.

15. John J. Duquette, "Forester's Experiment Evidence of Axton's History," *Adirondack Daily Enterprise*, March 25, 1995.

16. Charles Z. Lincoln, ed., *Messages from the Governors, X* (Albany: J. B. Lyon, 1910), 555, cited in *Education & Agriculture: A History of the New York State College of Agriculture at Cornell University*, by Gould P. Colman (Ithaca, NY: Cornell University Press, 1963), 161.

17. Charles Reznikoff, ed., *Louis Marshall, Champion of Liberty: Selected Papers and Addresses* (Philadelphia: Jewish Publication Society of America, 1957), 1020.

18. James G. Lewis, "The Pinchot Family and the Battle to Establish American Forestry," *Pennsylvania History: A Journal of Mid-Atlantic Studies* 66, no. 2 (1999): 143, accessed August 30, 2021, http://www.jstor.org/stable/27774186.

19. Schenck and Butler, *Cradle of Forestry*, 77.

20. Schenck and Butler, *Cradle of Forestry*, 116.

21. Schenck and Butler, *Cradle of Forestry*, 117–18.

22. Schenck and Butler, *Cradle of Forestry*, 20.
23. Lewis, "The Pinchot Family," 155–56.
24. Lewis, "The Pinchot Family," 156.
25. Gifford Pinchot, *Breaking New Ground*, 152.
26. Schenck and Butler, *Cradle of Forestry*, 118.
27. Schenck and Butler, *Cradle of Forestry*, 118.
28. United States Forest Service, "Yale Summer School of Forestry (1900–1926)," accessed September 4, 2021, https://www.fs.usda.gov/detailfull/greytowers/aboutgrey-towers/history/?cid=stelprd3824718&width=full.
29. Gifford Pinchot, *Breaking New Ground*, 152–53.
30. Forest History Society and Cradle of Forestry in America Interpretive Association, *First in Forestry*, 24:50–24:59.

CHAPTER 14: MACKAYE CHARTS HIS COURSE

1. Harvard College, record for Emil Benton MacKaye, class of 1900, UAIII 15.75.10mf, box 1.
2. Larry Anderson, *Benton MacKaye: Conservationist, Planner, and Creator of the Appalachian Trail* (Baltimore: Johns Hopkins University Press, 2002), 25.
3. Anderson, *Benton MacKaye*, 34.
4. Anderson, *Benton MacKaye*, 37.
5. Larry Anderson, "A Classic of the Green Mountains: Benton MacKaye's 1900 Hike Inspires Appalachian Trail," Hut2Hut, October 6, 2015, accessed September 22, 2021, https://www.hut2hut.info/a-classic-of-the-green-mountains.
6. James Sturgis Pray, "New Swift River Trail and Its Bearing on the Club's Policy," *Appalachia: Journal of the Appalachian Mountain Club* 10 (1902–1904): 173.
7. Anderson, *Benton MacKaye*, 43.
8. Dorothy M. Martin, "Interview with Benton MacKaye," *Potomac Appalachian Trail Club Bulletin* 22 (January–March 1953): 12.
9. Anderson, *Benton MacKaye*, 42.
10. Martin, "Interview with Benton MacKaye."
11. Anderson, *Benton MacKaye*, 43.
12. Benton MacKaye to James MacKaye, October 20, 1903, box 157, folder 13, Correspondence: Benton MacKaye to James Medbery MacKaye and wife, 1898–1954, MacKaye Family Papers, Rauner Special Collection Library, Dartmouth College.
13. "Forestry as a Profession," *Harvard Crimson*, March 2, 1900, accessed September 23, 2021, https://www.thecrimson.com/article/1900/3/2/forestry-as-a-profession-pmr-gifford.
14. Pray, "New Swift River Trail," 178.

CHAPTER 15: GIFFORD PINCHOT'S DEPARTMENT

1. Gifford Pinchot, *Breaking New Ground* (1947; repr., Seattle: University of Washington Press, Americana Library Edition, 1972), 145.
2. Elting Elmore Morison, ed., *The Letters of Theodore Roosevelt: The Years of Preparation, 1868–1900*, vol. 2, *1898–1900* (Cambridge, MA: Harvard University Press, 1951), 1421.

3. Harold T. Pinkett, *Gifford Pinchot, Private and Public Forester* (Chicago: University of Illinois Press, 1970), 54.

4. Gifford Pinchot, *Breaking New Ground*, 188.

5. Theodore Roosevelt, *December 3, 1901: First Annual Message*, National Archives, University of Virginia, Miller Center, Presidential Speeches, accessed October 12, 2021, https://millercenter.org/the-presidency/presidential-speeches/december-3-1901-first -annual-message.

6. Roosevelt, *December 3, 1901: First Annual Message*.

7. Gifford Pinchot, *Breaking New Ground*, 191.

8. Gifford Pinchot, *Breaking New Ground*, 254, 260.

9. William L. Hall, "Hail to the Chief," *Journal of Forestry* 43 (August 1945): 566.

10. USDA, "Forest Preservation and National Prosperity: Portions of Addresses Delivered at the American Forest Congress, January 2 to 6, 1905, by President Roosevelt, Ambassador Jusserand, Secretary Wilson, and Others," Circular No. 35, 5–8.

11. USDA, "Forest Preservation and National Prosperity," 8.

12. Gifford Pinchot, *Breaking New Ground*, 254, 260.

13. Gifford Pinchot, *Breaking New Ground*, 261.

14. Gifford Pinchot, *Breaking New Ground*, 261.

15. Gifford Pinchot, *The Use of National Forest Reserves: Regulations and Instructions*, U.S. Department of Agriculture, Forest Service, Washington, DC, June 13, 1905.

16. Ralph S. Hosmer, interview by Elwood R. Maunder, September 26, 1960, Forest History Society, 13, accessed October 15, 2021, https://foresthistory.org/wp-content /uploads/2016/12/HOSMER60.pdf.

17. Bibi Gaston, *Gifford Pinchot and the First Foresters: The Untold Story of the Brave Men and Women who Launched the American Conservation Movement* (New Milford, CT: Baked Apple Club, 2016), 183.

18. Gaston, *First Foresters*, 63.

19. Gifford Pinchot, *Breaking New Ground*, 282.

20. Gifford Pinchot, *Breaking New Ground*, 293.

21. Pinkett, *Gifford Pinchot*, 76–77.

22. Congressional Record, 59th Cong., 2nd Sess., vol. 41, part 4, February 23, 1907, 3722.

23. Gifford Pinchot, *Breaking New Ground*, 300.

24. Gifford Pinchot, *The Fight for Conservation* (New York: Doubleday, Page, 1910), 79.

25. Gaston, *First Foresters*, 115.

26. *Denver Republican*, April 29, 1909, cited in Pinkett, *Gifford Pinchot*, 70.

27. Gifford Pinchot, *Breaking New Ground*, 281.

CHAPTER 16: HETCH HETCHY

1. Gifford Pinchot, *Breaking New Ground* (1947; repr., Seattle: University of Washington Press, Americana Library Edition, 1972), 100.

2. Gifford Pinchot, *Breaking New Ground*, 103.

3. Karen Wonders, "Big Trees as Trophys," Institute for the History of Science, accessed October 17, 2021, http://www.cathedralgrove.eu/text/05-Pictures-Politics-4.htm.

4. "Giving a Dam: Congress Debates Hetch Hetchy," History Matters, accessed October 17, 2021, http://historymatters.gmu.edu/d/5721.

5. *Hetch Hetchy Reservoir Site Hearing before the Committee on Public Lands*, U.S. Senate, 63rd Cong., 1st Sess., on H.R. 7207, An Act Granting to the City and County of San Francisco Certain Rights of Way in, over and through Certain Public Lands, the Yosemite National Park, and Stanislaus National Forest, and the Public Lands in the State of California and for Other Purposes (printed for the use of the Committee of Public Lands; Washington, DC: U.S. Government Printing Office, 1913), 39.
6. Roderick Frazier Nash, *Wilderness and the American Mind*, 5th ed. (New Haven, CT: Yale University Press, 2001), 135.
7. Holway R. Jones, *John Muir and the Sierra Club: The Battle for Yosemite* (San Francisco: Sierra Club, 1965), 94.
8. Horace M. Albright and Marian Albright Schenck, *Creating the National Park Service: The Missing Years* (Norman: University of Oklahoma Press, 1999), 316.
9. John Muir, "The Yosemite," *Century Magazine*, 1912, 249–62.
10. "Giving a Dam."
11. "Giving a Dam."
12. Nash, *Wilderness*, 162.
13. John Muir to Robert Underwood Johnson, January 1, 1914, quoted in Nash, *Wilderness*, 180.

CHAPTER 17: THE CHIEF IS DISMISSED

1. Gifford Pinchot, *Breaking New Ground* (1947; repr., Seattle: University of Washington Press, Americana Library Edition, 1972), 392–93.
2. Gifford Pinchot, *Breaking New Ground*, 396.
3. Gifford Pinchot, *Breaking New Ground*, 398.
4. Gifford Pinchot, *Breaking New Ground*, 406.
5. Louis R. Glavis, "The Whitewashing of Ballinger: Are the Guggenheims in Charge of the Department of the Interior?," *Collier's*, November, 1909, 15.
6. Gifford Pinchot, *Breaking New Ground*, 427.
7. Gifford Pinchot, *Breaking New Ground*, 438.
8. Gifford Pinchot, "Conservation and Equal Opportunity," People's Forum, New Rochelle, New York, 1909.
9. Gifford Pinchot, *Breaking New Ground*, 449.
10. Harold T. Pinkett, *Gifford Pinchot, Private and Public Forester* (Chicago: University of Illinois Press, 1970), 129.

CHAPTER 18: THE NATIONAL FORESTS COME EAST

1. National Forest Reservation Commission, *A Report on Progress in Establishing National Forests* (published on the fiftieth anniversary of the Weeks Law, U.S. Department of Agriculture, Forest Service, 1961), 3.
2. Lincoln Bramwell and James G. Lewis, "The Law That Nationalized the U.S. Forest Service," *Forest History Today*, Spring/Fall 2011, 11.
3. Bramwell and Lewis, "The Law," 10.
4. Julius H. Ward, "White Mountain Forests in Peril," *Atlantic Monthly*, February, 1893, 248.
5. Ward, "White Mountain Forests," 248.

6. Charles D. Smith, "The Mountain Lover Mourns: Origins of the Movement for a White Mountain National Forest 1880–1903," *New England Quarterly* 33, no. 1 (1960): 41, https://doi.org/10.2307/362963.

7. Bramwell and Lewis, "The Law," 10.

8. Christopher Johnson and David Govatski, *Forests for the People: The Story of America's Eastern National Forests* (Washington, DC: Island Press, 2013), 18.

9. Bill Gove, *J. E. Henry's Logging Railroads* (Littleton, NH: Bondcliff Books, 1998), 107.

10. Larry Anderson, *Benton MacKaye: Conservationist, Planner, and Creator of the Appalachian Trail* (Baltimore: Johns Hopkins University Press, 2002), 74.

11. Bramwell and Lewis, "The Law," 8.

12. National Forest Reservation Commission, *Report on Progress*, 9.

13. Bramwell and Lewis, "The Law," 15.

CHAPTER 19: ALONG COMES THE NATIONAL PARK SERVICE

1. Horace M. Albright and Marian Albright Schenck, *Creating the National Park Service: The Missing Years* (Norman: University of Oklahoma Press, 1999), 33.

2. Mather Homestead, Stephen Tyng Mather biography, accessed October 27, 2021, https://www.matherhomestead.org/stephen-mather.

3. Albright and Schenck, *Creating the National Park Service*, 35.

4. Albright and Schenck, *Creating the National Park Service*, 60.

5. Albright and Schenck, *Creating the National Park Service*, 75.

6. Albright and Schenck, *Creating the National Park Service*, 75.

7. Albright and Schenck, *Creating the National Park Service*, 76.

8. Albright and Schenck, *Creating the National Park Service*, 81–82.

9. Albright and Schenck, *Creating the National Park Service*, 82.

10. Paul Sutter, *Driven Wild: How the Fight against Automobiles Launched the Modern Wilderness Movement* (Seattle: University of Washington Press, 2002), 102.

11. National Park Service, Act to Establish a National Park Service (Organic Act), 1916, accessed October 27, 2021, https://www.nps.gov/foun/learn/management/upload/1916%20ACT%20TO%20ESTABLISH%20A%20NATIONAL%20PARK%20SERVICE-5.pdf.

12. Albright and Schenck, *Creating the National Park Service*, 143.

13. *Report of the Director of the National Park Service for the Fiscal Year Ended June 30, 1921 and the Travel Season 1921* (Washington, DC: U.S. Government Printing Office, 1921), 15.

14. *Report of the Director of the National Park Service*, 26.

15. Albright and Schenck, *Creating the National Park Service*, 127.

16. Sutter, *Driven Wild*, 140.

CHAPTER 20: MACKAYE'S HISTORIC PATH

1. Larry Anderson, *Benton MacKaye: Conservationist, Planner, and Creator of the Appalachian Trail* (Baltimore: Johns Hopkins University Press, 2002), 143–44.

2. Paul Sutter, "'A Retreat from Profit': Colonization, the Appalachian Trail, and the Social Roots of Benton MacKaye's Wilderness Advocacy," *Environmental History* 4, no. 4 (October 1999): 565.

3. Benton E. MacKaye, "An Appalachian Trail: A Project in Regional Planning," *Journal of the American Institute of Architects* 9, no. 10 (October 1921): 5.

4. MacKaye, "An Appalachian Trail," 5.

5. Benton E. MacKaye, Address to the Southern Appalachian Trail Conference, May 26, 1934, Appalachian Trail Conservancy Archives.

6. Resolution adopted at the Southern Appalachian Trail Conference, May 27, 1934, Appalachian Trail Conservancy Archives.

7. Hal Goldman, "James Taylor's Progressive Vision: The Green Mountain Parkway," *Vermont History: The Proceedings of the Vermont Historical Society* 63, no. 3 (Summer 1995), 158.

8. Goldman, "Green Mountain Parkway," 169.

9. P. Jeffrey Potash, "The Green Mountain Parkway, 1933," Vermont History, accessed September 27, 2021, https://vermonthistory.org/green-mountain-parkway-1933.

10. Benton E. MacKaye, "Flankline vs. Skyline," *Appalachia: Journal of the Appalachian Mountain Club* 20 (1934): 104.

11. MacKaye, "Flankline vs. Skyline," 107.

12. Editor's note, *Appalachia: Journal of the Appalachian Mountain Club* 20 (1934): 104.

13. Larry Anderson, *Benton MacKaye: Conservationist, Planner, and Creator of the Appalachian Trail* (Baltimore: Johns Hopkins University Press, 2002), 270.

14. Benton E. MacKaye, "Why the Appalachian Trail?," *Living Wilderness*, no. 1 (September 1935): 7.

15. MacKaye, "An Appalachian Trail," 4.

16. Anderson, *Benton MacKaye*, 280.

17. Robert Marshall, "The Problem of the Wilderness," *Scientific Monthly* 30, no. 2 (1930): 148.

CHAPTER 21: VOICES FOR THE WILDERNESS

1. Stanley Temple, Senior Fellow, Aldo Leopold Foundation, interview by Jeffrey Ryan, June 21, 2018.

2. Aldo Leopold, cited in Paul S. Sutter, "'A Blank Spot on the Map': Aldo Leopold, Wilderness, and U. S. Forest Service Recreational Policy, 1909–1924," *Western Historical Quarterly* 29, no. 2 (1998): 210, https://doi.org/10.2307/971329, from Aldo Leopold, "A Wilderness Area Program" (about 1922), series 10, subseries 6, folder 4, box 16, Leopold Papers.

3. Joe Paddock, *Keeper of the Wild: The Life of Ernest Oberholtzer* (St. Paul: Minnesota Historical Society Press, 2001), 151.

4. Paddock, *Keeper of the Wild*, 160.

5. Oberholtzer quote from oral history, cited in Paddock, *Keeper of the Wild*, 161.

6. Paddock, *Keeper of the Wild*, 178.

7. Robert Marshall, "The Problem of the Wilderness," *Scientific Monthly* 30, no. 2 (1930): 141–48.

8. Sutter, "A Blank Spot on the Map," 199.

9. Marshall, "The Problem of the Wilderness."

10. James M. Glover, *A Wilderness Original: The Life of Bob Marshall* (Seattle: Mountaineers, 1986), 145.

11. David M. Cole, "Planned Diversity: The Case for a System with Several Types of Wilderness," *International Journal of Wilderness* 17, no. 2 (2011): 9.

CHAPTER 22: A NEW SOCIETY

1. Harold Anderson to Benton MacKaye, October 14, 1932, cited in Larry Anderson, *Benton MacKaye: Conservationist, Planner, and Creator of the Appalachian Trail* (Baltimore: Johns Hopkins University Press, 2002), 237.
2. Paul Sutter, *Driven Wild: How the Fight against Automobiles Launched the Modern Wilderness Movement* (Seattle: University of Washington Press, 2002), 178.
3. Harold Anderson to Guy Frizzell, cited in Anderson, *Benton MacKaye*, 272.
4. Harvey Broome, "Origins of the Wilderness Society," *Living Wilderness*, no. 5 (July 1940): 11.
5. Benton MacKaye, "Invitation to Join the Wilderness Society," Washington, DC, October 19, 1934, Rauner Special Collections Library, Dartmouth University.

CHAPTER 23: DRIFTING ALONG

1. Richard L. Neuberger, "He Was a Millionaire Who Walked Himself to Death—Bob Marshall's Money Enshrined the Wilderness He Deeply Loved," 88 Cong. Rec. A430S, *Proceedings and Debates of the 77th Congress Second Session* (July 27, 1942–December 16, 1942).
2. Larry Anderson, *Benton MacKaye: Conservationist, Planner, and Creator of the Appalachian Trail* (Baltimore: Johns Hopkins University Press, 2002), 170.
3. Edward Zahniser, interview by Jeffrey Ryan, June 7, 2018.
4. Mark Harvey, *The Wilderness Writings of Howard Zahniser* (Seattle: University of Washington Press, 2014), 204.
5. Zahniser, interview.
6. Zahniser, interview.
7. Zahniser, interview.
8. Edward Zahniser, "Preserving Wilderness and Wildness as Enlarging the Boundaries of the Community," Wilderness Connect, accessed October 6, 2021, https://wilderness.net/learn-about-wilderness/howard-zahniser.php.
9. Zahniser, interview.
10. Edward Zahniser, "Wilderness in the Eternity of the Future" (speech at the Kelly Adirondack Center of Union College in Schenectady, New York, May 8, 2014), accessed October 6, 2021, https://wildernesswatch.org/keeping-wilderness-wild-blog-post/wilderness-in-the-eternity-of-the-future.
11. Zahniser, "Wilderness in the Eternity of the Future."
12. "The Black River Dam War," Adirondack.net, accessed October 6, 2021, https://www.adirondack.net/history/black-river-dam-war.
13. Zahniser, "Wilderness in the Eternity of the Future."

CHAPTER 24: MAN WITH A MISSION

1. Doug Scott, *The Enduring Wilderness* (Golden, CO: Fulcrum, 2004), 40.
2. USDA Forest Service, "The First Century," accessed October 7, 2021, http://www.pshistory.com/publications/usfs/fs-650/sec6.htm.

3. USDA Forest Service, "The First Century."

4. Scott, *The Enduring Wilderness*, 42.

5. Benton MacKaye, letter to Wilderness Society members, Washington, DC, November 9, 1947, cited in the *National Wilderness Preservation Act, Hearings Before the Committee on Interior and Insular Affairs*, U.S. Senate, 85th Cong., 1st Sess., on S. 1176 (June 19 and 20, 1957), 195.

6. Edward Zahniser, interview by Jeffrey Ryan, June 7, 2018.

7. Scott, *The Enduring Wilderness*, 43.

8. C. Frank Keyser, "The Preservation of Wilderness Areas, an Analysis of Opinion on the Problem," Legislative Reference Bureau, Washington, DC, 1949.

9. Tom Turner, *David Brower: The Making of an Environmental Movement* (Oakland: University of California Press, 2015), 62.

10. Michael Gordon and Karen Saffle, "History of the San Gorgonio Wilderness," San Gorgonio Wilderness Association, accessed October 13, 2021, https://sgwa.org/about/history-of-the-san-gorgonio-wilderness.

11. David Brower, "San Gorgonio Auction, Going, Going, —," *Sierra Club Bulletin* 32 (January 1947): 3.

12. Gordon and Saffle, "History of the San Gorgonio Wilderness."

13. Howard Zahniser, "Wilderness Preservation," *Land Policy Review*, Summer–Fall 1947, 8, 11.

14. Zahniser, "Wilderness Preservation," 11.

15. Kenneth Brower, interview, *62 Years*, film, dir. Logan Bockrath, accessed October 7, 2021, https://www.62yearsfilm.com.

16. Turner, *David Brower*, 75.

17. David Brower and Charles Eggert, *Wilderness River Trail*, 1953, film, accessed October 7, 2021, https://envhumanities.sites.gettysburg.edu/environmental-journalism/uncategorized/if-a-picture-is-worth-a-thousand-words-then-video-is-worth-a-million.

18. Turner, *David Brower*, 75.

19. Ann Gilliam, ed., *Voices for the Earth: A Treasury of the Sierra Club Bulletin, 1897–1977* (San Francisco: Sierra Club Books, 1979), 337.

20. Turner, *David Brower*, 78.

21. Jon N. Cosco, *Echo Park: Struggle for Preservation* (Boulder, CO: Johnson Books, 1995), xv.

CHAPTER 25: A WILDERNESS FOREVER

1. Doug Scott, *The Enduring Wilderness* (Golden, CO: Fulcrum, 2004), 45.

2. Howard Zahniser, "The Need for Wilderness Areas," *Living Wilderness*, no. 59 (Winter–Spring 1956–57): 43–58.

3. Edward Zahniser, interview by Jeffrey Ryan, June 7, 2018.

4. Douglas W. Scott, *A Wilderness-Forever Future: A Short History of the National Wilderness Preservation System* (Campaign for America's Wilderness, 2001), 15, accessed October 12, 2021, https://winapps.umt.edu/winapps/media2/wilderness/toolboxes/documents/awareness/Doug%20Scott-A_Wilderness-Forever_Future-history.pdf.

5. Mark Harvey, ed., *The Wilderness Writings of Howard Zahniser* (Seattle: University of Washington Press, 2014), 205.

6. Zahniser, interview.

7. Harvey, *Wilderness Writings*, 146.
8. Harvey, *Wilderness Writings*, 147.
9. Harvey, *Wilderness Writings*, 197.
10. Harvey, *Wilderness Writings*, 194.
11. Harvey, *Wilderness Writings*, 164.
12. David Brower, "The Constant Advocate," cited in Harvey, *Wilderness Writings*, 203.
13. "Compromising the Wilderness," *New York Times*, May 8, 1964, 32.

Chapter 26: Legacy

1. Howard Zahniser, Speech to the Western Federation of Outdoor Clubs, April, 1961, cited in Mark Harvey, *The Wilderness Writings of Howard Zahniser* (Seattle: University of Washington Press, 2014), 196.
2. "Saying Yes to Wildlands AND Woodlands" (seminar, December 17, 2020), accessed December 21, 2021, https://www.youtube.com/watch?v=vofpTvGvOW8.
3. Northeast Wilderness Trust, "Places We Protect," accessed December 21, 2021, https://newildernesstrust.org/places-we-protect.

Appendix: Invitation to Join the Wilderness Society

1. Invitation to Join the Wilderness Society, Washington, DC, October 19, 1934, Rauner Special Collections Library, Dartmouth University.

Appendix: Excerpts from the Wilderness Act

1. The Wilderness Act stats, accessed November 1, 2021, https://wilderness.net/learn-about-wilderness/fast-facts/default.php.
2. The Wilderness Act, accessed November 1, 2021, https://wapps.umt.edu/winapps/media2/wilderness/NWPS/documents/publiclaws/The_Wilderness_Act.pdf.

INDEX

Italicized page numbers indicate illustrations.

About the Author

Maine-based author, historian, and speaker **Jeffrey Ryan** has a passion for exploring the outdoors on foot and along the dusty paths of history. His travels on thousands of miles on both America's most famous and lesser-known trails have inspired several books and a documentary film project titled *Voices of the Wilderness*.

When he is not researching, writing, or hiking, Ryan can be found exploring the back roads of the USA and Canada in his vintage 1985 VW camper. Learn more at JeffRyanAuthor.com.